"… a particularly happy place"

A history of
Lady Margaret School
1917-1992
and of its predecessor
Whitelands College School
1842-1917

by
Brian H. Owen
BA(Hons) MA(Ed)
Head of English Department

Published on the occasion of the 75th and 150th
anniversaries of the two Schools

LADY MARGARET SCHOOL
Parson's Green
London SW6 4UN

1992

"Two little ones from the Kindergarten presented a bouquet . . ." Bishop Maud and Dr Lyttelton are sitting either side of the Princess.

Cast of the Pageant detailing the history of Belfield House, June 6th 1918. Irene Lovett is in front, holding a fan; Hazel Russell on the right.

The Pageant, June 6th 1918. Behind the wall is Elm House.

The Pageant, June 6th 1918. A view of the audience. The close-cropped man in front is Dr Lyttelton, and the elderly lady clutching a picture of Lady Margaret Beaufort is Princess Christian.

Beginnings

Belfield House on Parson's Green has seen a great many comings and goings in its long history. Nikolaus Pevsner, in his Buildings of England series, dates the house as the beginning of the 18th century, but it is certainly earlier. (When repairs were being done, in 1948, to the wall adjoining Lupton House, "an old timbered wall, probably of 16th century construction", was found.) Belfield is a modest symmetrical red-brick edifice, built in that style now known as Queen Anne. Mrs Jordan, the mistress of the Duke of Clarence (later King William IV), lived here for some time, and her royal lover no doubt was an occasional visitor. But on Thursday December 6th, 1917, there was another royal visitor, the Princess Marie Louise, daughter of HRH the Princess Christian, deputising for her recently widowed mother. The Princess (Queen Victoria's granddaughter) was there to open a new school.

The event had been planned for November 15th, but the death of Prince Christian, and the period of formal mourning which followed it, had made that impossible. The Head Mistress, Miss Enid Moberly Bell, had chosen the name "Lady Margaret School" for the new venture, calling to mind that great benefactress of education, the mother of King Henry VII, who had founded St John's and Christ's Colleges at Cambridge.

The occasion went well. Two little ones from the Kindergarten presented a bouquet, the whole School sang a song of welcome, speeches were made, and (for this was a strongly Church of England school) prayers were said and a hymn sung. Everyone had tea, the Princess looked round the garden, and then was driven off in her car with the cheers of schoolgirls ringing in her ears.

The following summer, Princess Christian herself was able to keep her appointment. On Thursday June 6th, 1918, she was regaled with a specially devised pageant detailing the history of Belfield House and its various famous inhabitants. Little Pixie Ward, of the Lower School, made a speech, and then Hazel Russell, the Head Girl, in her role as the Lady Margaret Tudor, acted as chorus for the ensuing pageant. Finally, Bunty Skelton, aged six and a half, of the Kindergarten, made a presentation, the National Anthem was sung, and so the day ended.

These very English proceedings, unremarkable in many ways, were in fact very remarkable indeed. The nation was embroiled in the darkest days of the Great War. For three years the blood had flowed like water across Europe, and even as Lady Margaret School celebrated its birth, a generation of young men were dying in the muddy horror of Passchendaele. Money was short, and new schools for girls were a long way down the list of most people's priorities. Miss Moberly Bell and her small band of helpers were well aware of the War, and kept their young charges aware of it as well. However, the sacrifice of the nation's youth, far from being a reason why their venture should not go ahead, was part at least of the reason why they were determined to succeed. The new school was a personal crusade to preserve and foster the very essence of those values for which they felt the nation was fighting.

For preservation it was. When the new school opened its doors on September 19th, 1917, it was in fact not so very new at all. The senior pupils and the staff certainly knew each other well, and had been working together for several years already, at the Whitelands College School in Chelsea. When that association was threatened in the early part of the year, those who valued it felt strongly that they had to find some means of preserving it, and the opening of Lady Margaret School was the culmination of six months' frenzied activity that must often have seemed hopeless. In her speech to Princess Marie Louise, Miss Moberly Bell said:

> "I think it is the kindness and friendliness we meet on all sides that makes Lady Margaret School a particularly happy place..."

Nine months earlier, in March 1917, she had known nothing of "a particularly happy place" called Lady Margaret School. For the reasons for her unhappiness, and the events that followed, we need to go back another 75 years, to the beginning of the reign of Queen Victoria, and the foundation of the Whitelands College School in Chelsea.

Chelsea Dawn

Early in the 19th century the concern of the Church of England for the education of the masses resulted in the setting up of charity schools. The National Society "for the Promotion of the Education of the Poor in the Principles of the Established Church" was formed, and in 1811 it assumed responsibility for these schools. To staff the schools, the Society set up a central teachers' training establishment. Soon this Central School proved quite inadequate for the task, and the decision was taken to provide such training facilities in each diocese; London itself was to have two central colleges. Both were established in Chelsea, a men's college, St Mark's, towards the Fulham end of the King's Road, and a women's in a three-storied Georgian house near Sloane Square, called "Whitelands".

Whitelands House is shown clearly on Horwood's 1799 plan of London. It stood facing north on the south side of the King's Road, just to the west of the Duke of York's Royal Military Asylum; opposite it was a large nursery garden, behind which stood another house, called Blacklands, at the end of what is now Marlborough Road, but was then Blacklands Lane. (The significance in this colourful opposition of names I have been unable to discover!) It was by contemporary report a beautiful house, with a delightfully ornate wrought iron front gate complete with link extinguishers incorporated into the design. (The gate has survived many vicissitudes, and is still preserved at Whitelands College in Putney.) It already had quite a lengthy connection with education, having in the latter half of the 18th century been a school where the Rev. John Jenkins, MA, had lectured on "Female Education and Christian Fortitude under Affliction", and when in 1841 the National Society took out a 99-year lease on it (paid for by a bequest from the Rev. Wyatt Edgell of North Cray, in Kent), the girls' boarding school run by the two Miss Babingtons had just closed.

A Lady Superintendent was appointed to the newly formed College, a Scottish widow, Mrs Julia Field, and she was there to receive the first students in January 1842. In the early years of the College, the teaching staff were augmented by some of the local clergy, who came to teach divinity, the chaplain of the new St Mark's College, the Rev. Derwent Coleridge (son of the famous Romantic poet), and the Rector of near-by St Luke's Parish Church, Chelsea, the Rev. Charles Kingsley (father of the author of *The Water Babies*), among others.

At first, the students of Whitelands did their teaching practice at the Chelsea Parochial Schools, in King Street, the proximity of which had been the reason for setting up the two colleges in the area. This arrangement soon proved unsatisfactory, and the first of the Whitelands schools, a commercial school for girls, was opened in 1842 within the college buildings, where students could practise and observe more conveniently. The school began with just twelve pupils, who each paid 9d a week, or 10/6d a quarter, in fees. In 1843 an infants' school was opened, to be followed in 1844 by the Model School, a National School taking girls at the reduced rate of 4d a week. By 1855 there were three, and later four, schools, each with a certificated Head Teacher under the superintendence of the College Mistress of Method.(This awesomely designated official was simply the college tutor in charge of the professional, as distinct from the academic, training of the students.)

From the beginning there was a great deal of interaction between school and college. Staff were often common to both, and teachers at the school were able to move into and up the College hierarchy. Pupils at the school would move on to become students at the College, and often move back again into the School as teachers. One such was Kate Stanley, who attended the College from 1856 to 1857. After a year in a school in Hampshire she returned to Whitelands to teach in the Infants' School. She became a governess (tutor) at the College, and was Head Governess from 1876 to 1902.

> *She was a particularly gifted teacher of needlework and gave much of her time to the chapel. Every student came into contact with her, but none more dramatically than Therese la Chard who was rebuked loudly by the Head Governess for wearing a straw boater, with the college ribbon round it, to church when her usual hat had been spoilt by rain. Kate Stanley's words of rebuke were used by the student decades later as the title of her autobiography, "A Sailor 'at in the 'ouse of the Lord."*
> (Whitelands College: The History. Malcolm Cole. 1982)

She continued to take an interest in both College and School after her retirement; she distributed the prizes at the 1911 Drill Display, and was usually among those on the platform at Prize-givings.

Chelsea Days

Afascinating glimpse of the daily life of school in those distant times may be had from an article by a former pupil writing in the Camden House Guild Magazine for May 1914, and reprinted in the Whitelands College School Magazine for 1915 (No.8, pp 16-18). It minutely describes her education in the National School in the mid-1860s.

At School - 1863-6

I was nine years old when I first went to a real school. It was at Whitelands Training College, Chelsea. As it was very unlike a modern school it may interest some members of the Guild if I describe it.

The School-room was long and narrow, with bare boards and whitewashed walls, and windows with ground glass panes high above our heads. Down one side of the room were rows of long desks and forms joined together, rising one behind the other; on the other side were the Head Mistress's table and chair. Before each set of desks stood an easel and blackboard and a large box containing slates, copy books, etc. Five or six girls sat on each form. Between each set there was a narrow passage and a curtain. Doors at each end of the room led to passages and class-rooms. There were no pictures, no piano, no seats for the teachers, no colour, except that the desks, originally white unpainted deal, had become dark grey and polished from long use and many elbows. The forms were narrow and without backs, but so arranged that we could lean against the desks behind.

No one thought then of open-air schools. Indeed, it was impossible to see out of the windows unless they were open. I think they could only be opened at the top, and then we saw a strip of sky and the branch of a cherry tree waving. Outside the School-room was a large and beautiful garden where we were invited to play and drink tea once a year. I do not think we really played, the occasion was too solemn! We walked about, holding each her own cup, and admired the flowers in whispers until we were collected and told to sing grace. Then we seated ourselves on the lawn, and the cups which we had brought from home were filled with milk and water, and each child had a bun - Nectar and Ambrosia! I, for one, look back on these feasts with great joy. We thought them heavenly at the time.

We never dreamed of playing, or even talking, in school hours, though below the School-room was a kind of paved cellar with arches opening into the "Earthly Paradise". This cellar was called the play-ground, but a child must be high- spirited indeed who could frisk there. Besides, we never had time. The cloak room, large and airy, was at one end of this play-ground, and through the arches we could some-times see the teachers walking in the garden.

School began at 9 o'clock. The first half-hour was spent in repeating lessons we had learned by heart; a column of spelling and a table every day; the Collect and Gospel of the preceding Sunday, on Monday; Geography, i.e., the Counties of England, on

"The Earthly Paradise".

Tuesday; Poetry on Wednesday (the School religion was strictly Evangelical, therefore, officially, we learned no poetry except Cowper's Task); on Thursday, the Catechism; and on Friday, dates and tables. We said these lessons one by one to a long-suffering teacher, and filled up the remaining time with writing dates and tables on our slates. Sometimes we made rhymes, e.g.,

> *"William in mud his hands did fix,*
> *In the year ten hundred and sixty-six."*

But if that crime were discovered, we were kept in to write dates and "wives" properly.

At 9.30 a bell rang and we stood at attention while the Head Mistress, Miss Pearman, entered and walked with slow and stately steps to her table. She was distinguished from the other teachers by wearing an enormous crinoline (they had none) which gave her great dignity and importance in our eyes. After surveying us for a moment, she said, "Be seated", but almost immediately after, "Stand!" Then, striking a tuning-fork, she started a hymn in which we all joined, read prayers, then settled down, each with our own teacher, to a Scripture lesson, except on Wednesday, when she took the upper-half of the School into one of the class-rooms and gave the lesson herself. I have had many good teachers since then, but never one who was so dramatic and interesting. She made us see without pictures. Everyone of the Old Testament heroes was a living man to us, and each had her favourite. Mine was Jeremiah. We were expected to write full reports of these lessons at home, and often I wrote till my pen dropped from my fingers, and I had to let my mother finish from my dictation. Miss Pearman took the other half-school on another day. On Thursday the half-school went into the class-room again for the last hour and then she gave us a lesson on some special subject, such as an incident in History, or Travels, or some natural object. In these lessons we picked up phrases, and for days would "take umbrage" and accuse each other of "behaving unseemly". These, with the weekly singing lesson (tonic sol-fa) were the only classes Miss Pearman took herself, but she walked from class to class, and watched the teachers, and now and then would take a class herself to our great delight. Each lesson from a teacher lasted half-an-hour, and between each we sang and sometimes marched. We were very carefully taught to read aloud and learned most of our History and Geography from our books, but we also read specimens from other literature. We had Arithmetic and Writing (Copies and Dictation) every day.

At about 11.45 our clothes were brought up in baskets and silently distributed and put on, and while this was going on we learned our "unofficial" poetry. Miss Pearman shared my taste for stirring poems. She would say a few lines which we repeated. In this way we learned a good part of "Marmion", "The Lady of the Lake", "Lay of the Last Minstrel", "Lochiel's Warning", "The Inchcape Rock", and many others. At 12.0 we sang grace and went home. We had to form an orderly "caterpillar" to the end of the road, but afterwards we dispersed. At noon we went straight home, but in the afternoon we escorted each other, the whole party going out of its way to deposit A, and then accompanying B, till I, who lived at the greatest distance, was left alone.

We were back again at 2 o'clock and sat sewing in utter silence till 3.30. Our sewing was severely plain, except in the fortnight before the Christmas Holidays, when we were allowed to do fancy work. Before I left we heard that Miss Pearman was going to be married, and that those who could sew well enough would be invited to make her underclothes. You may imagine the competition. Even her new stockings were darned all over the sole, one thread up, two down, in a pretty zig-zag pattern. But this unhappy one who writes, pricked her finger at an early stage, and could not share in the honour and glory. After sewing we marched and sang for quite a long time, then read and wrote till 4.30, when we sang our evening hymn and said our prayers, learned some more poetry, and went home.

Lent was a hard time. Every Friday afternoon the Rector and the Curate conducted a service. As the Rector was old and afraid of cold every window was shut, and all through the Morning Prayer and the Litany we had to kneel on those hard narrow benches. The only relief was when we stood up to sing; the only excitement was wondering who would faint. Somebody always did.

We were an orderly set on the whole; still, punishment was sometimes necessary. The most common was having to stand out either by the teacher's easel, or more terrible, in the middle of the room by Miss Pearman's table. Sometimes, for very flagrant offences, the Head Mistress would slap each side of a girl's face with loud awe-inspiring smacks. I was told by Rosina Henfry, who had opportunities of knowing, that, except for the noise, it did not hurt a bit. Rosina and Felicity Henfry were curly-headed, red-haired twins, always in mischief, always in trouble. When one was punished the other cried. We thought this remarkable.

On wet days those who lived more than half-a-mile away were allowed to bring their dinner. This was dreary work. Perhaps there would be three or four unfortunates. We ate our sandwiches in the big empty room, and then tackled the long division sums that our teacher had thoughtfully provided for our delectation. If we spoke our voices echoed horribly. Once Anne Hurst ran screaming up and down the room (she called it "jodelling"). It was terrible. For the most part we sat quietly miserable, feeling very grubby, for though there was some water, there were no towels or basins. How we watched the clock, and decided that next time we would get wet twice before we stayed to dinner. Saturday was a holiday, so- called. We had extra home lessons, and some of us, I among them, had French and music lessons at home. Madame Fragonard taught both. She was fat and very sleepy. I repeated long passages from the "Echo de Paris". If I stopped she murmured "Encore" and went to sleep again. She taught music in the same way. I did not enjoy those lessons.

On reading this over it seems to me an account of rather a hard life, but at the same time we thoroughly enjoyed it. We liked the routine and the strict discipline, and we loved and venerated our Head, Miss Pearman. In the summer her desk was hidden in flowers. Once or twice she came to tea with us, and talked to my mother like an ordinary person. She even came without her crinoline and told fairy tales.

B. R.

Shades of Lowood and little Jane Eyre!

Chelsea Sunset

In the 1880s the National School was closed, and in 1890 the Whitelands College Council decided to streamline the organisation and administration of the remaining schools by placing them all under the one Headmistress, who would also be the College Mistress of Method. Miss Hebblethwaite was appointed to this new position. Under her, in each of the three departments, was an assistant mistress who acted as Head of her particular department. Miss Gregory became head of the Upper School, Miss Pinnock of the Lower School, and Miss Culverhouse of the Infants'.

This was a period of considerable change in the educational scene in England. Many schools, Whitelands among them, were, often through pressure of parents' wishes, extending their courses to increasingly older children. The Bryce Report of 1895 recognised the pressing need for a systematic organisation of Secondary Education in order to put right some of the anomalies of the existing chaos, chief among which was the fact that local authorities were not allowed to spend public money on pupils above elementary school age (usually 13), and therefore local authority schools which were retaining pupils beyond this age found themselves in a difficult position; they received no public money for such pupils, nor were they allowed to charge fees for their support. The recommendations of the Report were finally put onto the statute book in the Education Act of 1902, after a great deal of controversy, particularly from the Nonconformist churches, who objected to their rates and taxes being spent on the Church schools which had been incorporated into the national system; many of their members withheld their rates in protest, and were sent to prison. However, as a result of the Act, Whitelands became one of the newly recognised secondary schools in which London County Council scholarships could be held. (These enabled children from LCC elementary schools to study at secondary schools free of charge or at reduced rates.)

Miss Hebblethwaite died in October 1906. A portrait was commissioned and hung in the School Hall. Her chief commemoration, however, was the institution of the Hebblethwaite Memorial Literature Prize, awarded annually to the best performer in a truly formidable examination of English and Western European authors. Three one-and-a-half hour papers, covering Prose, Poetry, and General Literature, with a lengthy and weighty reading list issued beforehand, ensured that the winners earned their prize of a set of books specially bound in red calf. The last two prize-winners, in 1915 and 1916, were Phyllis Ruegg and Dora Fisher, who, though they left Whitelands before the transfer to Parson's Green, were to become the staunchest of "instant" Old Girls of Lady Margaret School.

The Chapel at Whitelands.

Miss Hebblethwaite was succeeded, in accordance with her wishes, by Miss Gregory, destined to be the last Headmistress of Whitelands School. Edith Gregory was by all accounts a formidable woman. She was of an older generation of teacher, lacking the academic background of some of her younger staff - Girton, Newnham, Lady Margaret Hall. She had trained as a teacher at Whitelands in the 1880s and subsequently gained a Silver Medal from the Royal Apothecaries' Society; she was not a graduate, but she knew where she wanted her girls to go. Irene Lovett (Mrs Fraser) (Whitelands 1914-17, Lady Margaret 1917-19) recalls the terror of her admission interview. She had made the mistake of preceding her mother into Miss Gregory's study, and not holding the door open for her, and was there and then subjected to a long lecture on politeness and the deference due to one's elders, which had her face in flames and her whole being quaking in her boots. (Fortunately, she seems otherwise to have made a good impression, for she was awarded one of the coveted LCC Junior County Scholarship places, her father, a butler, being unable to find the full fees charged by the school, by then five guineas a term.) This first view of the redoutable Miss Gregory was reinforced upon further acquaintance.

> Our Headmistress was a martinet of the old school. We were terrified of her, though I believe her Sixth Form appreciated her as they came to know her better. So far as we juniors were concerned, she simply froze us with a look - she would begin at our toes, work up, and then back again. By that time we were as worms ready to sink into the earth. I well remember one unfortunate in the Lower Fourth who dared to yawn during

Miss Gregory's maths lesson. "Beatrice, people only gape for three reasons - one is that they are tired, another that they are bored, and the third that they are hungry. Were you late to bed last night?" "No, Miss Gregory." "I cannot think that you are bored. So you must be hungry - go to the kitchen and ask Amy for a bun." Poor Beatrice!

(Amy was the School Maid, who had replaced her sister Minnie at Easter 1908 when she was married. Amy herself was married in 1915, and the last Whitelands Magazine, of 1916, records the arrival of a baby son, Donald.)

The school shared many facilities with the college, including the services of Regimental Sergeant-Major Elliott, the college Professor of Drill and the school Drill Master. (Some idea of the function and practice of a drill-master in a Victorian girls' school may be had from reading Gillian Avery's novel, *The Elephant War*.) These drill-masters were retired NCOs and Warrant Officers from the army, who instructed the nation's emerging womanhood in military drill and the new-fangled Swedish drill in order to inculcate discipline and a respectably upright carriage. There is an old photograph of Whitelands students doing incredible things with broomsticks (Cane Drill, it was called) while wearing full-length skirts and straw boaters. More advanced classes in "Swedish Gymnastics" took place across the way, using the staff and equipment of the Duke of York's Royal Military Asylum. Sgt-Major Elliott's death in May 1915, aged 89, is recorded in the School Magazine; he was clearly, despite everything, a well-loved figure.

The first annual Drill Display and Competition took place in Chelsea Town Hall, in July 1908, and every year thereafter. Items included the Mass Drill, consisting of free exercises, the Kindergarten Ring Drill, the Junior Step Marching, Dumb-bell Exercises, the Senior Step Marching, Flag Drill, Cane Drill, Junior Ring Drill, and Figure Marching. The competition was judged by Miss Bear, Principal of the Alexandra House Gymnasium, which was to drill what Aldershot was to boxing and Twickenham to rugby football.

Perhaps the most colourful common experience of College and School was the annual May Day celebration. At the instigation of William Morris, the founder of the Arts and Crafts Movement, the College had instituted a traditional May Day, with a May Queen elected from among the students, a procession, and much dancing and merry-making. (To this day Whitelands College still elect a May Queen, though, since it became a mixed college in the 1970s, May Kings are equally eligible!) The School was closely involved in these jollifications, electing a Rose Queen who, with her two maidens, attended the May Queen during the ceremonies. The Sixth Form was usually invited to witness the final rehearsals, and, of course, the entire School was granted a whole holiday on May Day itself.

The May Queen and her attendants.

Whitelands At Work

One of Miss Gregory's earliest innovations was the establishment of a School Magazine, in 1908, and a glance at its pages for those final years before 1917 show that Whitelands College School functioned in much the same way as did most girls' secondary schools in those days.

It was, first and foremost, a Church school, and on the major occasions, Ash Wednesday, Ascension Day, and the Harvest Thanksgiving on St Ursula's Day, there were services in the College chapel, built by the Rev. John Faunthorpe, the first College Principal, in 1881, and continually beautified thereafter; in particular there were the series of windows depicting women saints of the Church and the reredos which covered the east wall, both by William Morris. (The reredos and windows were removed to the new College at Putney, and can be seen in the Chapel there.) In 1911, Miss Luard, the College Principal, gave permission for the School to hold its daily morning service there instead of in the School hall. In 1914 was formed the School Guild, for all those who had been confirmed, which combined spiritual fellowship with charitable work. Ascension Day was, of course, a half-holiday, but in 1914 there was a new departure; the whole School (except for the Kindergarten) went to Richmond Park for a picnic, after the usual service in the chapel. The War put a stop to this at once, but the precedent was not forgotten; when the School was re-established at Parson's Green, the Ascension Day picnic became a regular feature of the annual round.

Shortly before the School's demise (or translation, perhaps) a house system was set up; Winifred Barnes, the Head Girl for 1916-17, and Kathleen Richards, her predecessor for 1913-15, in what was to be the last Whitelands School Magazine, wrote:

> During the Summer Term a new scheme was devised to enable our Sports to be run on more equal terms. On the old plan it was form against form - an obviously unfair division because of the difference in age and ability between the III and the VI form. The new plan has divided the School into four parts with a proportionate number of girls out of each form in each division. The divisions call themselves Orders, and each Order is named after one of the Saints in the Chapel Windows.
> We have the Orders of St Cecilia, St Dorothea, St Martha, and St Veronica.
> *(Whitelands School Magazine No.9, 1916)*

There was the annual Prize Day, held initially at the newly built Chelsea Town Hall, but in 1915 and 1916 in the School Hall. On this occasion notables like the Chairman of the College Council or the College Principal would present the prizes and certificates, and, in the best Public Schools tradition, pupils would be "put on" to recite. Dora Fisher (Mrs Pollard) (Whitelands 1911-1917) recalls that her rendition of the Horatian ode III.2 ("Dulce et decorum est pro patria mori"), during the last Town Hall occasion in November 1914, was not well received by one cleric on the platform because "as the new pronunciation was used he hadn't understood a word of it".

The girls exercised themselves at a variety of games, organised and financed, as was then the practice, largely by themselves. Hockey was introduced in the autumn of 1906.

> We obtained permission from the Head Mistress (the late Miss Hebblethwaite) to get up elevens from the Sixth and Fifth Forms, provided that we could obtain: firstly, a ground sufficiently close to the School; secondly, enough money to buy the necessary goal-posts and balls. We were lucky enough to fulfil both conditions, obtaining a very nice pitch in Battersea Park, within easy walking distance of the School.
> *(Whitelands School Magazine No.1, 1908)*

Cricket was also played, again by the VI and V Forms; the IV Form was given permission to join in, "provided that they could obtain another pitch". A tennis club was formed in the summer of 1908, and a swimming club. Finally, in the autumn of 1909, netball (for those seniors who did not wish to play hockey) and rounders (for the juniors) were added to the pantheon of games; the various sports were then united into one all-embracing Games Club. Because of the lack of facilities at the College, all games took place in Battersea Park, across the river, and the girls had to troop there on each occasion, in the inevitable crocodile, in full uniform. The first school Sports Day was held in the College garden on the last day of July 1915, "to which parents and friends were invited. No prizes were given, but a collection was made on behalf of the Belgian children in those parts of Belgium occupied by the Germans" (Magazine No.9, 1916).

Various other activities flourished. There was a Missionary Society, with senior and junior branches, which operated under the auspices of the Society for the Propagation of the Gospel, whose Secretary for Girls' Schools, Miss Moberly, a cousin of Miss Moberly Bell's, was a frequent visitor. The Debating Society discussed such motions as "The Vote should be granted to Women, on the same basis as to Men". The Cercle Francais too had debates on the same topic, as well as readings from Moliere. The German Club, set up in 1911, did not, of course, survive the outbreak of war three years later. The Field Club went on rambles across the neighbouring parks and commons, and along the tow-path at Kew. The London Club exercised itself in visiting and studying the historic sites of the capital.

There was a strong tradition of drama. An open-air performance of Thackeray's *The Rose and the Ring*, in July 1907, was followed in succeeding years by *A Midsummer Night's Dream* (1909), *As You Like It* (1911), *The Pied Piper of Hamelin* (1912), and Longfellow's *Hiawatha* (1913); all these took place in the "Earthly Paradise", the College garden, a magical *al fresco* setting pre-dating Regent's Park by several decades! In the spring of 1913 there was a performance of *The Rivals*, and in the summer the Juniors presented a French play, *Le Petit Chaperon Rouge*; French plays were clearly popular, for at the December 1913 Prize-giving there was a performance of a scene from Moliere's *Les Femmes Savantes*, and Ascension Day in 1915 was marked by the performance of *Les Precieuses Ridicules*.

Whitelands had a good academic reputation; Phyllis Ruegg (Hebblethwaite Memorial Prizewinner for 1915 and tennis captain in her last year) went up to Newnham College, Cambridge in 1916, and a regular stream went on to university and training college courses. That this was the case was undoubtedly due to the staff, who, academically speaking, were a formidable bunch. The Senior Assistant Mistress, Enid Moberly Bell, who came to the school in 1911, had studied at Newnham. She was the sombre figure (her father had recently died, and she was in mourning) that young Dora Fisher was most impressed by on her first day:

> *Dominating the row of staff assembled on the platform was a tall figure in black - identified later as Miss Enid Moberly Bell.*

Hazel Russell, who went on to become the first Head Girl at Lady Margaret, recalls:

> *She always stood out as a unique personality to be reckoned with, but refused to believe us later when we assured her she inspired awe without effort. As a teacher, of course, she was herself inspired; I do not remember her ever giving a dull lesson, and when I think of the books she succeeded in persuading us to read, outside the curriculum, I am confounded.*
> (Lady Margaret School Magazine 1966-67)

The Staff of Whitelands College School, July 1917. Miss Gregory is seated, middle; on her right, MB.

Marcia Hartley, an M.Sc. from Liverpool University, appointed to Whitelands in 1907, taught science, and Mary Frances Phillips (known as "Bliss" by everyone) (Lady Margaret Hall) taught Latin and Religious Studies. Emily Woodhouse was another Newnham woman, and taught mathematics. Miss Laughton, with a Teachers' Certificate from South Kensington, was the Art Mistress. Other members of staff included Miss Dunell (Girton), and the three Kindergarten teachers, Miss Moore, Miss Harmsworth, and Winifred Pidwell, whom Miss Bell, on arriving at Whitelands in 1911, found "slightly alarming", until she "discovered that her correct exterior was only a kind of shyness which concealed a most generous and friendly nature".

The school had a rather smart (and "strict and protective", remarks Dora Fisher) uniform of navy blue drill slip ("2 inches below the knee") tied at the waist with a girdle, cream shirt and blue and gold striped tie, gloves, and a straw boater with a blue and gold ribbon on which was the school badge, a bishop's mitre; in the summer, white dresses were worn. It enjoyed considerable prestige, yet despite this it remained small (fewer than 200 pupils, of all ages 5 to 18) and financially insecure. One reason for this must have been the poor accommodation, which had hardly altered since 1863.

> *We had a Hall lower than the level of the street, and the rooms were all rather dark and had windows very high up, so that you could not see out of them. We had not any playground, except one side of the College garden, and the children had to be quiet there, because the school hours did not match with college hours, and any noise in the garden disturbed the students' work.*
> (History, 1926)

One change that had been made merely aggravated the general discomfort; towards the end of the nineteenth century, the local council had built a men's urinal onto the side of the school, on the corner of Walpole Street - it can be clearly seen in postcard views of the College taken at the time. This addition to the local amenities hardly improved the salubriousness of the site; in the summer it smelt to high heaven, and being without a roof was a source of embarrassment all the year around.

It is interesting to look through the Whitelands magazines to see those names which will later figure in the history of Lady Margaret. One does so posthumously. Miss Herbage, the Modern Languages Mistress since September 1911, died suddenly in January 1916, and as a memorial a number of reproductions of Renaissance artists were bought to adorn the walls of the School; these were among the few things which transferred to Parson's Green the following year. Olive Barnard won an Attendance Prize in 1913, and Vera Sutherland, Evelyn Gooch, and Muriel Sharp a prize each for Divinity in 1914. Hazel Russell (the first Head Girl at Lady Margaret) gained both a Form Prize and the Junior Musical Dictation Prize in 1914. A large map of the world, for the best essay on the work of the Navy League, was won by Irene Lovett.

Whitelands College in the King's Road. The men's lavatory can be clearly seen.

The coming of the Great War in 1914 brought some changes to the daily routine of school life. Dora Fisher recalls:

> *The King's Road - my twice daily trek between home near the World's End and school - was transformed first by the flood of Belgian refugees; then soon after by groups of convalescent soldiers from the 4th General Hospital at St Mark's College in their uniform of bright blue tunics and trousers, white shirt and red tie. Hallos between them and school girls added excitement to the trek and not a little anxiety to the staff.*
>
> *Wartime school was invaded by army grey wool for sock knitting. Miss Moberly Bell would knit continental style without ever glancing at it while she taught the rule of sonnet making or analysis or essay writing.*

The Head Girl, Kathleen Richards, noted in the Magazine:

> *Our School, like everything else, has been considerably affected by the War. One has only to walk through the garden at Recreation or at Lunch Time to know that something extraordinary has happened, for there are everywhere signs of unusual diligence which generally takes the form of sock or mitten knitting....*
>
> *The School has been very busy, too, providing for refugees. Every Friday evening during the Winter Terms a work party for the Senior School was held, and on this account most of the School Societies have discontinued their meetings. Needlework lessons, through most of the School, were immediately turned to good account in making clothes for refugees, and at home and in odd moments girls have been working for our Sailors and Soldiers with the result that the School has turned out over two hundred pairs of socks for the Troops, besides a large quantity of mittens, helmets, mufflers, etc., for the Sailors.*
>
> *It will be seen by this that the War has not been an unmitigated evil for the girls of Whitelands, since it has made us all think much less of ourselves and much more of other people.*　　　　　　　　(Whitelands School Magazine No.8, 1915)

One way in which this spirit of sacrifice manifested itself was at the annual Prizegiving; in lieu of a prize, each successful girl received a certificate, while the value of her prize was sent to the Red Cross.

The War provided a novel form of competition for the new "Orders":

> *During the War each Order has undertaken some definite war work. St Cecilia is finishing off jerseys and other garments knitted by the blind, at the London Association for the Blind, who afterwards sell the articles; and knitting socks. St Dorothea is making bags for the personal possessions of the wounded in hospital; and knitting socks. St Martha knits socks and sends magazines to the soldiers. St Veronica helps at the Chelsea Branch of the Surgical Requisite Association on Wednesday afternoons, and knits for the soldiers.*　　　　　　　　(Whitelands School Magazine No.9, 1916)

There were other shadows lowering over Chelsea, however, besides the Great War. The whole site in the King's Road was cramped, for the College as well as the School, play space very limited for the two hundred or so pupils, and the need not to disturb the College students always a curb on girlish high spirits. From the College's point of view there had been for some time some grave concerns over the school, which the War, and the growing requirements of the College, merely exacerbated, and in 1917 matters suddenly and (for some) devastatingly came to a head.

The Gathering of the Clouds

The first intimation that all was not well came at the College Council meeting on October 11th, 1916, when the Headmistress's Report declared a deficit of £240.0s.11d at the end of the school year just finished.

> *The Chairman pointed out that the question of the future of the School was one which would have to engage the serious attention of the Council in the near future.*
> (Minutes of Whitelands College Council)

There were at this time just 184 pupils, and these numbers had not changed for several years. Room for expansion, which would have been the most obvious way to improve the financial situation, was simply not available at Whitelands; the College itself had ambitions to grow, and these and the School's long-term welfare seemed mutually exclusive. A ray of hope appeared when (as was recorded in the minutes of the Council meeting on February 14th, 1917) the London County Council suggested that the School be recognised as a Pupil Teacher Centre, and offered to draft a letter for the Board of Education to that effect, if the College Governors were agreeable. The Council agreed that the School should be so recognised. The LCC had its reasons for this apparently altruistic move. The majority of the pupils at the School were in fact LCC Scholarship holders, and therefore the authority were in some sense responsible for what went on there; one thing that they did not like was the comparatively low pay of the Staff. Clearly, however, the College Council's agreement was little more than a gesture, for at the same meeting

> *The question of the future of the School was discussed and it was agreed that the matter should be referred to a Sub- Committee. (Minutes)*

A month later to the day, on March 14th, the Council met again to consider the report of the sub-committee, which had moved with commendable haste; clearly, if something were to be done, it had to be done quickly. The report was brutally clear and to the point. The number of pupils had been static for the past five years; the majority of them were LCC Scholars paying the reduced rate of fees. Moreover, despite a high degree of efficiency, there was a growing deficit in the School account; the estimated total loss by July 31st was £400. (In fact, it turned out to be nearer £800). The LCC had "severely criticised" the College for the scale of teachers' salaries, and threatened to withdraw their pupils unless the salary levels were increased. Again, and perhaps most importantly, the School was in fact of little further use to the College as a Practice or Demonstration School. (The students at the College were for the most part training as Elementary School teachers, and they needed much larger classes to practise on, rather than the cosy small classes offered by the Whitelands School, and a much less academic curriculum than that of a girls' secondary school. The 1870 Education Act had created many suitable elementary schools in the district for the students to practise in, while the 1902 Act had seen to it that Whitelands' own school had become increasingly unsuitable!) Finally, the Board of Education was constantly pressing for additional accommodation for the College, and in this they were supported by the National Society, which backed the use of the School facilities by the College. (Already, in 1908, the Kindergarten had been moved out of its room in the main building - which then became the College Art Room - into a new building in the garden; there was little possibility of continuing this process.)

So the Sub-Committee reached its recommendations. The School should close on July 31st, 1917. The Headmistress, Miss Gregory, should receive six months' notice from March 25th, and the other staff a term's notice. With such scant regard, seventy-five years of girls' education at Whitelands was to be brought to an end.

Miss Gregory seems to have accepted the situation as final; she was receiving much better terms than the rest of the staff, and perhaps she felt that some of the blame for the state of things must be hers, for she had had the running of the School, when all is said and done. Her assistants, however, were made of sterner stuff; Girton, Lady Margaret Hall and Newnham turned out giants in those days. They could see the logic of the College's position; and working daily in the cramped and run-down building they knew the unsatisfactory nature of the site. But the parents had found something there for their daughters that they valued, and they protested very vehemently, and with equal logic, that Church people ought not close down a Church school. They approached Miss Moberly Bell, recognising in her the steel that Miss Gregory, no longer young, did not have, and asked her rather fiercely what she was going to do about it. MB and the rest of the staff were convinced that a Church Secondary School for girls should continue in the area; the parents wanted it, the girls wanted it, and Enid Moberly Bell and her colleagues wanted it. But how it was to be done was not at all clear. She later wrote in her own History of Lady Margaret School:

> *As soon as people heard of the decision of the Council they began to ask, "Aren't you going to do something about it?" It is so easy to say that, and so difficult to see what to do. 1917 was a very bad year in the War. It was very difficult to get any building done, and it seemed almost impossible to think of finding a big empty house. Still, it seemed that one must try to do something.*

Rescue Plans

Enid Moberly Bell was a devout Churchwoman, as were the rest of her staff. She undoubtedly believed in miracles, and in Divine intervention in the deeds of men - and women. She suggested to Miss Gregory that if they could find a suitable building and get some promises of financial support they could approach the College Council again; Miss Gregory thought there could be no harm in trying. And so it was to be. The Whitelands College Council had met to hear the findings of the Sub-Committee on March 14th, 1917.

> *On March 18th some of my form were being confirmed at St Dionis' Church by the Bishop of Kensington, John Maud. Miss Phillips and I were going up to the Confirmation so I wrote and asked the Bishop if he could spare me a few minutes after it. He took me into the Rectory, and told the Vicar's wife he wanted to talk business with me; we were left alone and I told him all about the proposed closing of the School. We talked it all out, and he said it certainly must not be allowed to happen; he felt that probably we could raise enough money to save it, but that the real difficult was to find a building that was possible. We had just reached this point when Mrs Carter, wife of the Vicar of St Dionis, came in to see if we were ready for tea, and seeing our depressed expression asked if she could help us. "I'm afraid not," the Bishop said, "unless you can tell us of a house big enough to hold a school." "Well," she said, "I can. There's Belfield House opposite."*   *(History, 1926)*

Here, perhaps, was the answer to a great many fervent prayers. MB was not one to let the grass grow under her feet.

> *We went and looked over the house the very next day. It did not then look as it does now. It was much more beautiful. There was a lovely open oak staircase that went up from the Entrance Hall to a landing ... The Wing which now contains the laboratory was then broken-down stables. We saw at once that the house would do, and having seen that, we had to find some money to buy it with.*   *(History, 1926)*

And find it they did. "Whitelands parents, friends of the Staff, people who cared about Church education, all contributed." However, the greater part of the money, £2000, came from a close friend of Miss Moberly Bell's mother, Miss Gertrude Carver, whose family was to be among Lady Margaret's greatest benefactors. (The Carver family had been prominent and highly successful businessmen in Egypt when the Moberly Bells lived there, and the acquaintance then made had blossomed into a much stronger relationship; they were also cousins.)

The next step was to obtain a stay of execution from the College until the new premises could be made ready to receive the School. The plan at this point seems to have been that Whitelands would continue to be responsible for the School on its new site, since their main point of concern had been that they needed the School premises at the Chelsea site. These were now available, a new home had been found for the School, and Mr R B Barron, who had been assisting in the business arrangements for the purchase of Belfield, was now commissioned to make the formal approach to the College Council, offering them the building and the continuing administration of the School.

There followed a great deal of toing and froing, and some measure of the activity may be gleaned from the business of the College Council meeting on May 9th. On that occasion, members were informed of the rapid developments since their last meeting on March 14th.

> *The Chairman stated that immediately after the last Meeting of the Council, representations were made to him of strenuous efforts that were being made by friends of the College School for its continuance in a large house & grounds which could be acquired at Parson's Green, and he was desired to request the LCC to take no action upon the decision to close the School till after the College Council Meeting on May 9th. The LCC Higher Education Committee had consented to postpone action till then.*
>
> *The Chairman also stated that, acting on the request of many friends of the School, he had convened a Meeting of the Sub- Committee (appointed to enquire into the School question) together with one or two other persons. At this Committee Miss Moberly Bell, Senior Assistant Mistress of the College School, was present and stated that, through the support of influential friends, the house at Parson's Green had already been purchased and that a Council had been formed for the purpose of carrying on as a Church of England Secondary School for Girls and that funds were being generously promised or lent without interest.*

The original plan, that Whitelands should continue to administer the school, was not to be.

> *The Chairman stated that he had consulted the Chairman and other Directors of the Church Schools Co. as to the possibility of their taking over and continuing the School under their direction and there seemed reasonable expectation that they might do so. But he had received a report from Mr Burrows, consulting Architect to the National Society, only just in time to present to the Sub-Committee on April 18th. That careful Report stated that only at very considerable outlay (even if then) could the buildings be converted into a Public School for girls to meet the minimum requirements of the Board of Education and the LCC and that in his (Mr Burrows') opinion it was unsuitable even for a private school. This report seemed in the opinion of the Committee to preclude any further action by the Council of Whitelands College in the promotion of the scheme for the resuscitation of Whitelands College School in these new premises.*

The indomitable Enid's response rings out even from the cold formality of the Whitelands College Council Minutes Book!

> *Miss Moberly Bell then stated that she & her friends would nevertheless persevere in the scheme and that it would be carried on by its Council as a Private Venture School.*

Unfortunately this move precluded the School from receiving any financial assistance from the Society for the Promoting of Christian Knowledge, which had been one of the sources of possible funding of the project. Since it was not clear in what sense this would be a Church School (since Whitelands no longer managed it), they were reluctant to commit themselves.

Nevertheless, MB pressed ahead, with the "support of influential friends". To assist her in her seemingly madcap and impossible task she had gathered together a Governing Body for the embryonic school that included eminent educationists, well-placed politicians, and leading journalists - her family had long had close connections with The Times newspaper. Mr Barron had written to a number of concerned and energetic people to ask them to support the venture by joining the Council. The Bishop of Kensington of course was a member, and was appointed President. Mr Barron, an Old Etonian, recruited the Hon. Dr Edward Lyttelton, formerly Headmaster of Haileybury, and, until the previous year, Headmaster of Eton. Dr Carter, the Vicar of St Dionis', was another. Viscount Dunluce (soon to succeed his father as Earl of Antrim), who was highly placed in the Ministry of Munitions (the government department which would need to be approached over any building plans), was clearly a useful ally. Another Etonian connection was Mr Ernest Wythes, who had been a sterling worker on the Eton War Memorial Committee. Mr (later Sir) George Parkin, a notable educationist who had assisted in the administration of the Rhodes Scholarships, was also persuaded to lend his support to the school. The Hon. Miss Mary Pickford was later to become a Member of Parliament. Mrs Moberly Bell had been a keen supporter of her daughter's school at Chelsea, arranging outings for the pupils and appearing on the platform at Prize-giving (perhaps some of this was reflected glory from her late husband) and obviously she had a very personal involvement in the success of MB and her venture. Miss Gertrude Carver we have already mentioned; she and Mrs Bell were staunch supporters of girls' education and of Christian education.

Dr Lyttelton was appointed Chairman of the new body, and it was he who next took up the cudgels. The new Council met for the first time on May 7th, and its members were informed that

> *...a new house was found at Parson's Green which could be adapted to hold 250 girls. Miss Carver and Miss Moberly Bell arranged to buy the freehold property, a house and close upon one acre of land for the sum of £2250.*
>   *(Lady Margaret School Council Minutes, May 7th 1917)*

MB was appointed Headmistress, and the level of fees fixed at 65/- a term maximum. (These were soon raised to four guineas a term.) A list of requests was also passed, to be put to the College Council; these were considered at their May 9th meeting.

> *The Chairman further stated that he had just received a letter dated May 7th from Counc. the Hon. E. Lyttelton, Chairman on behalf of the Committee of Management of the projected new school, making the following four specific applications to the Council of Whitelands College -*
> 1. *That the Council of Whitelands College would approve of the use of the name "Whitelands" for the new School.*
> 2. *That the new School might be allowed the use of the present School furniture until the end of the war.*
> 3. *That the Council of Whitelands College would inform the LCC that the School was*

to be reopened at Parson's Green in September, by which time they expected to be recognised by the Board of Education.

4. *That in the event of the alteration of the new buildings not being completed by September, the Whitelands Council would allow the new School, working under its own Council, the use of the present School buildings.*

Clearly, in the forefront of the minds of all those concerned with the school was the absolute necessity to maintain continuity; if there were any faltering, the pupils would be dispersed, and the venture would come to a premature end. The College Council, for their own good reasons, we may be sure, were less than enthusiastic in their response.

These four points were very carefully considered and discussed and the Chairman was requested to inform Dr Lyttelton that:

1. *The Council decline to approve of the name "Whitelands School" being adopted by the new school, on the ground of the inconvenience and confusion with Whitelands College which would arise.*

2. *The question of the use of the School furniture until after the war was deferred for investigation and consideration.*

3. *He had been desired by the Council to inform the LCC that a new School would probably be opened at Parson's Green in September next under a new and distinct Governing Body and that Miss Moberly Bell had been appointed Head Mistress, with other members of the present School Staff as her Assistants.*

4. *The Council much regret that they are unable to see their way to any further occupation of the School buildings which are urgently needed by the College.*

The End of Whitelands School

The refusal to allow the old name of the School to continue was a blow; perhaps more than anything else, the name "Whitelands" would have signalled to the world that the good work of seventy- five years was continuing, and that the College felt sufficiently confident of its offspring that it was happy to acknowledge it publicly as its own. The reservation on the grounds of "confusion" can hardly be taken seriously; King's College School, University College School, Stockwell College School, were all in existence without any problems arising. Perhaps the serious doubts as to the new school's viability, clearly expressed at the Council meeting, made the College anxious that it should incur no extra expense during those very difficult years towards the close of the War. Then there was the personal problem of Miss Gregory; she was not strong physically, and no longer young; she was certainly the last person to be put in charge of so uncertain a venture, which would require energy and vision if it was to succeed. It was difficult to imagine, moreover, the LCC agreeing to the continuance of a non-graduate as the Head of a secondary school, and the College perhaps could not face the task of appointing someone else over the head of one who had served them loyally for so many years. Whatever the reason, there is no mistaking the College's intention. The Sub-Committee meeting on July 17th accepted the following statement of principle:

> It was further emphasised that, as there is no continuity between the Whitelands School and the new school which is to be opened at Parson's Green, in the disposal of any of the School property care must be taken not to take any action which would be seen to establish or imply such continuity.

There is not a mention of Parson's Green in the article on the closure of the School in the latest edition of the Whitelands Annual Journal, and the school reports issued in July 1917, as the girls dispersed for their summer holidays, have a line drawn through where the date of the new term was normally entered.

Meanwhile, the activities of MB and her friends had come to the notice of the local press.

> An interesting scheme is on foot to transfer the Secondary School for Girls from Whitelands College, King's-road, to Parson's Green. An official notice, dated July 3rd, reminds us that the School has hitherto been housed in a wing of the well-known King's-road College. Now further accommodation is required for student-teachers and the Council governing the establishment are therefore obliged to close the School. Still, the institution is one of the very few Church secondary schools in London and serves the districts of Fulham, Chelsea, Clapham, and Battersea. If its work were discontinued altogether parents would be obliged to find places for their children in schools where education would not be based on religion. Accordingly an effort is being made to establish the new Whitelands School at Parson's Green. (Fulham Chronicle, July 6th 1917)

That "effort" was by now prodigious. Whitelands itself was clearly not of a mind to assist overmuch in the new venture, and the future of the school must depend upon the strenuous activity of its supporters. A prospectus was issued, frankly appealing for money.

> A very suitable house has been found at Parson's Green. The ultimate cost of buying the freehold, adapting the house, moving into it, etc., will amount to £7,000, but not more than £5,000 need be incurred at present. Of this £2,800 has already been subscribed, and a confident appeal is made to Church people for their support and interest.

Further difficulties were yet to come. At the College Council meeting on May 9th, it was resolved to defer consideration of the disposal of the school furniture to a later date. The Sub- Committee meeting on July 17th were read a letter from MB, in which she made offers for certain of the Whitelands School properties for use in the new school. Again the College was less than enthusiastic in its willingness to assist in the safe delivery of its troublesome child.

In her letter to the Council MB asked for all the stationery in stock; this was refused. She asked for the sets of school text books; she was told that any that the College did not want she might have "at 3d a volume or at a fair second-hand price", but the name of Whitelands College was to be removed from the books - otherwise they should all go for waste paper or to second-hand dealers. The school desks she could have, "at a valuation"; likewise the science equipment, "except for the balances". The Kindergarten apparatus was to be retained by the College for demonstration purposes by the Method Tutors. Of the five pianos, two were to be retained by the College, the other three being disposed of to a dealer for £25. All the school trophies - shields, cups, presentation pictures - were to be kept by the College, and placed in the former School Hall at Whitelands "as a memorial to the School". Of the books in the School Lending Library, some were to be kept by the College, the rest given to Miss Gregory "for use in her new sphere of work". Finally, the School Prayer Book (which without doubt would have meant a great deal to MB) was to be given to Miss Gregory.

A last decision by the Sub-Committee at that depressing meeting was to wind up the School Endowment Fund; all remaining monies were to be returned to the donors. Whitelands College School had ceased to exist.

Form V B, Whitelands College School, July 1917. Irene Lovett is the second from left, middle row. The Form Mistress is Miss Phillips.

Whitelands College School. The last photograph, July 1917.

Phoenix from the Ashes

Before it was swept up in the sprawl of modern London, Parson's Green was a small hamlet situated just outside the old Fulham settlement, later to become Fulham Town. Parson's, or Parsonage, Green derived its name from its close position to the Fulham Rectory House [this stood where St Dionis' Church now is] and had an appealing rural character which was highlighted in its annual fair. The fair was established in the reign of William III and enjoyed great popularity until its suppression in 1823. "At that time besides the rows of booths arranged under the trees on the east side of the Green ... might be seen the usual concomitants of an ancient country fair such as greasy-pole climbing, treacle bobbing, ale-broaching, and competitive hot-tea drinking." The fair had acting booths, puppet shows, and refreshments, and at the tip of the Green there were fish stalls selling oysters and whelks; people came from all over London to the fair, and its suppression was met with great dismay.

At the south east end was a large pond fed by a natural spring. Colepitts, as it was known, was occasionally visited by the neighbouring Baptists who immersed their members in it. "Dogs and Ducks patronized it and the market gardeners led their horses into it to bathe." When the main drainage for the New King's Road was laid, the natural spring was destroyed and the pond filled up; shops and part of the road now stand on part of its site. Parson's Green was said to be inhabited "mostly by Gentry and Persons of Quality" but occasionally had to suppress its hardened criminals: in 1476 Alice Parker was brought to court because she allowed a pig to cause havoc "upon the Common of the Lord called psenage-grene". (Magazine, 1978-79)

Parson's Green has a great many historical associations. South-east of the Green, on the other side of the New King's Road, stood Brightwells, which dated back to the fourteenth century. It later became known as Parson's Green House, and, in 1633, when Thomas Carey was in occupation, as Carey House, or Villa Carey. His daughter Elizabeth married Sir John Mordaunt, who later came into ownership. Their son, Charles Mordaunt, was in 1697 made Earl of Peterborough, and Villa Carey became Peterborough House, and latterly Grove House. It too was demolished, at the beginning of this century, and the Peterborough Estate was built.

In 1754 Samuel Richardson, auther of "Pamela" and "Clarissa", moved here from his house, The Grange, in the North End Road; he lived in a house at the south-west side of the Green (next to the Duke of Cumberland public house) previously inhabited by Sir Edmund Saunders, Lord Chief Justice until 1683. The house was demolished in 1805, and Gosford House and Arragon House built on the site. Arragon House owes its name to the fact that Catharine of Aragon, the lately divorced wife of King Henry VIII, had a house on or near the site.

On the other side of the Green, on the block between Delvino Road and the present school, stood what was originally called Hollybush House, but later East End House. Robert Blanchard owned it in 1666; he left it to his wife in 1681, who in turn passed it on to Sir Francis Childs when he married their daughter in 1685. Sir Francis was a member of the famous banking family, which came to own much of the property on and around Parson's Green. He died in 1715, and the house was leased to Sir Charles Wager, First Lord of the Admiralty. Later, from 1808 to 1810, Mrs Maria Fitzherbert, the "unofficial" wife of the Prince Regent (later King George IV), lived here. In the latter part of the century the notorious "Squire" Daniel occupied the house, which was demolished in 1884.

Belfield House, to the north of East End House, took its name from Squire Daniel's nephew, Mr Thomas Daniel Belfield, who lived there from 1825 to 1849. It and its neighbour, Elm House, stand on what was an ancient plot of land dating from the fourteenth century, originally called "Hore's", and later "Parlor's", tenement. An earlier house on the site was occupied by Sir John Vaughan, who played host to Lord Chancellor Francis Bacon when he was banished from Court and forbidden to approach anywhere near it. In 1617, Dr Thomas Iles, of Christ Church College, Oxford, bought the property, and built himself a cottage on the southern half of it, the part now occupied by Belfield House. Iles' Cottage then began its separate history, eventually becoming Belfield House. The nucleus of the present house is thought to be of mid-seventeenth century date, with some later additions. For a while, at the beginning of the nineteenth century, the Duke of Clarence (later King William IV) kept his mistress, Mrs Jordan, here.

Readers of stage memoirs may remember that this lady's real name was Dorothy Bland. At the age of 15 she made a great name for herself on the boards at Dublin, and subsequently appeared as "Peggy" in "The Country Girl" at Drury Lane. The Duke fell in love with her, and maintained an illicit relationship with her until 1811. By her Royal lover the popular actress had no fewer than ten children.

(Fulham Chronicle - 10th August 1917)

Finally, in 1890, the artist Theodore Roussel acquired Belfield. It was by then in a poor state of repair, and he restored and improved it. He had built onto the back a large studio, where he could do his work. (The site is now covered by the Physics laboratory.)

It was this house which, on that fateful day in March, 1917, MB pronounced "would do"; and when the Council of Whitelands refused any further occupancy of the school buildings at Chelsea beyond July, it was this house that she and her band of trusty allies strove feverishly to make ready not only for the start of a new term, but also for the start of a new school.

As to the name of the new school, it was a case of third time lucky. The original choice had been, as we know, "Whitelands School"; but the Council of Whitelands College refused consent for that. Then, at the Management Committee meeting held on June 11th, Dr Carter (the Vicar of St Dionis) and Miss Carver proposed that Buckingham Palace be approached for permission to use the name "The Princess Mary School", after King George V's daughter (our present Queen's aunt); the Princess had visited Whitelands only recently, for the May festival, and had delighted everyone by saluting the new May Queen with the customary kiss. Mrs Moberly Bell asked Princess Christian, whose friend she was, for her help in this, but the answer from the Palace was a polite "no" - it was too uncertain a venture to be patronised in this way. Instead, therefore, MB decided on that of a woman who in her time had given much to education; the Lady Margaret Beaufort, mother of King Henry VII, after whom Lady Margaret Hall at Oxford had been named, was to be the Patron of the new school. (MB's particular friend on the staff, Miss Phillips, was an alumna of Lady Margaret Hall, and she may well have suggested the notion to her in the first place.)

The local press followed developments with interest.

The Lady Margaret Secondary School for Girls is the title of the new seminary at Parson's Green. It is generally known that Whitelands School, Chelsea, has been disestablished, and that Belfield House, Parson's Green, is being transformed into a Church of England school to continue the work done at Whitelands.

(Fulham Chronicle, August 10th 1917)

The builder is putting the final touches to his work at Belfield House, Parson's Green, and on September 19th the establishment will be opened with the title of the Lady Margaret School for Girls....Although called "The Lady Margaret School", it is really a continuation of the work done at the Whitelands College School in the past; and the school will open on September 19th with practically the whole of the former staff and many of the old pupils.   *(Fulham Chronicle, September 14th 1917)*

"The builder" had certainly worked at the task, as well he might if MB's promise (first made in May in a letter to Whitelands parents to assure them that the School would be continuing) to open on the 19th was to be honoured. Fortunately, Mr Barnes was not just a builder. He was the father of Winifred Barnes, the last Head Girl at Whitelands, and of Sheila Barnes, who would be transferring to the new school (and who in her turn was to be Head Girl at Lady Margaret); and it was therefore both with a personal interest and with a wider concern to see the school succeed - in short, as one of that great army of friends that the school has always attracted - that he gave his services liberally to the adaptation of the house for its new purpose. MB later wrote:

When we began building operations, we were told that it would require a miracle to get this house turned into a School in time to open in September. It was accomplished, and the worker of this miracle was Mr Barnes. You can all see the building we owe to him; but you can't see his indefatigable energy, his untiring patience ....

(Magazine 1, 1917-18)

Others, too, had played their part in ensuring the success of the venture. Seventy-five pupils were eventually "rescued" from the old Whitelands; the LCC, following its refusal "to put the new school on the list of schools approved to take County Scholars" (Council Meeting Minutes, July 9th 1917), had removed all its Scholarship holders and distributed them among other schools. Those remaining to transfer were exclusively the fee-payers - with two exceptions. The Sixth Form at Lady Margaret seemed destined to begin with just four pupils in it. Miss Anne Lupton, with whom MB shared a house in Chelsea, and who was to be for the rest of her life a friend and generous benefactor of the school, offered to pay the fees of two of the LCC Scholars, to be chosen by MB for their promise and aptitude. Thus it was that Ruby Joselin and Irene Lovett ("a

very clever LCC child", as MB described her at the July 9th meeting), both still only fourteen years old, were not compelled to leave the school they loved, but instead became the youngest members of the new Sixth Form.

And so, finally, on September 19th as MB had promised, with the laboratory still unfinished and the paint still wet on the walls, with a large debt still outstanding and a World War still raging, with a minimum of resources but an excess of hopes and good wishes, buoyed up, no doubt, more by passionate conviction than by deep-seated certainty, with 86 girls and 11 little boys, the Lady Margaret School opened its doors upon the world.

Hazel Russell, first Head Girl of Lady Margaret School.

Idyll in Parson's Green

It is hardly possible to believe that we have completed our first year at Lady Margaret School; and as we look back over this first exciting year, I suppose the predominant feeling in all our minds is gratitude for all the help and encouragement we have received.

So wrote MB in the first number of the Lady Margaret School Magazine. She may be excused her amazement at the success of her venture, for although she had earnestly desired it, and strenuously sought after it, there must have been in her heart, as well as in the hearts of many who wished the new school well, a nagging conviction that "it would be all over by Christmas". But such prophecies had been made before, and proved wrong, and when after a year "The Lady Margaret School" was still up and running, was moreover growing rapidly in size, so that only a year after its birth it was not far short of the numbers of its predecessor, MB could be forgiven her very human whoop of exultation in the Magazine.

Contrary to the gloomy prognostications of all our friends, we opened on the day we had fixed - September 19th - with 95 children. By the end of the term we had risen to 111. We began the Easter Term with 132 and closed with 138, and we reached 150 shortly after the beginning of this term. (Magazine 1, 1917-18)

When those doors opened on 19th September, 1917, work on the reshaping of Belfield was still uncompleted. Even getting it started had been a struggle; the War was on, and any building project had to have a Priority Certificate to enable it to proceed. Getting this out of the Ministry of Munitions had been the particular task of MB's mother, who apparently besieged the Ministry's premises until, like the importunate widow of the Gospels, she was given it from sheer desperation. (It may have been of some additional help that Lord Dunluce, who worked in that Department, was also one of the School Governors!) The next problem was the shortage of building materials, but with Mr Barnes and his knowledge of the trade, that was managed as well.

So the School opened. Of the original staff at Whitelands, eight came on to Lady Margaret: Miss Moberly Bell, Miss Hartley, Miss Phillips, Miss Laughton, Miss Woodhouse, Miss Pidwell, Miss Benton, and Miss Milman. They were joined by Gladys Sharp, who had been a girl and then a student at Whitelands, and Miss Kirby, who taught French. There was as yet no cook/housekeeper, and until the arrival of the Thumwoods, for many years to act as a husband-and-wife team of schoolkeeper and housekeeper, Miss Sharp's mother (yet another from MB's apparently bottomless pit of friends) filled in for the first six weeks. (Her husband seems to have been part of the bargain, "always able and ready to produce coal and coke, or chairs, or anything else we have needed, at a moment's notice".)

Two other pillars of strength were the Rueggs, parents of Phyllis, who had left Whitelands School just before the move to Parson's Green to read Medieval and Modern Languages at Cambridge. Mrs Ruegg "knew all about accounts and filing and clerical work generally [and] she came up to school in the early days to show Margery Sharp....how to do the books. Mr Ruegg managed all our insurance affairs for us, and he has been a regular subscriber to the School from the beginning." (When Phyllis came down from Cambridge, she took over the Editorship of the School Magazine!)

The garden behind Belfield was still very much a garden. It was some time before the part of it nearest the house was asphalted over for a playground, but in the meantime the girls were able to enjoy, in their various seasons, bluebells, crocuses, lilac, laburnam, irises, roses, cornflowers, and syringa. As it was still war-time, the lower half of the garden was dug up for the growing of vegetables, and the school diet was being supplemented with its own onions, carrots, potatoes, artichokes, tomatoes, beans, peas, cabbages, rhubarb, turnips, spinach, and radishes.

Ten days after the opening, on September 29th, the Feast of St Michael and All Angels, the Bishop of Kensington celebrated Holy Communion in St Dionis' Church; and afterwards, in all his episcopal finery, he led a procession of staff, girls, parents, former Whitelands girls, and friends of the School, across the Green to Belfield to consecrate the house to its new purpose. Thereafter, St Michael was adopted as the School's Patron Saint and Michaelmas Day as the School Birthday, to be celebrated in various ways, but with unflagging enthusiasm, ever since.

Another Patron was HRH the Princess Christian, born the Princess Helena to Queen Victoria in 1846. She was a friend, as we have seen, of Mrs Moberly Bell, and it was at her own request that she became the School's Patron, and she and her daughter,

Princess Marie Louise (who lived to be the only surviving grand-daughter of Queen Victoria at the present Queen's coronation in 1953) took a keen and active interest in the School during its early years. Her son had been killed in the South African War, and her husband, Prince Christian, died just as Lady Margaret School was born. The opening ceremony was due to be performed by her on November 15th, but her husband's death prevented this, and her daughter came instead, on December 6th. On that occasion, Miss Lilian Faithfull, Head Mistress of Cheltenham Ladies' College, made an address of welcome to this latest recruit to the ranks of girls' schools. Princess Christian finally fulfilled her engagement the following June, when she was entertained by the first of the Pageants that the School was to present in the ensuing years.

Marjorie Clayton, one of the original Sixth Form, 1917.

The new school quickly established itself as a faithful successor to Whitelands. The four "orders" that had existed at the Chelsea site were continued, at the request of the girls, and St Cecilia, St Dorothea, St Martha, and St Veronica were soon vying with one another in inter-house sports on Ascension Day (St Veronica won), the collecting and displaying of picture postcards, and the elimination of litter about the school. This arrangement, however, seems not to have lasted long, for by the following year there is no further mention of it, and games were once again played between forms, as they had long been at Whitelands. A Literary Club was formed, which discussed among other works Charlotte Bronte's *Villette* and Jane Austen's *Emma*. The School adopted St Elizabeth's Home at Lavender Hill (an orphanage run by what was later to become the Church of England Children's Society) as its charity, and there were visits between the two institutions. The School Guild was re-established, dedicated to St Michael, instead of All Saints as it had been at Whitelands.

Clearly, the Whitelands connection was a strong one. All the senior girls were ex-Whitelands, and former Whitelands pupils were readily adopted as ready-made Old Girls of the new School; their comings and goings were duly reported in the School Magazine. (Many of them were engaged in active War Work, including nursing at the front in France.) Several of the continuing pupils of the School had sisters or mothers who had attended its predecessor, and it was the most natural thing in the world to treat them all as colleagues in the on-going venture. The Lady Margaret School Old Girls Association was formed as soon as the School itself, with its own hockey club, under the captaincy of Gladys Sharp, both a former Whitelands pupil and a member of the staff of the new school, who in addition had two sisters in the School. A very visible reminder of Whitelands was the collection of pictures obtained from the Herbage Memorial Fund, which were used to decorate the form-rooms at Parson's Green.

Margaret Brice, one of the original Sixth Form, 1917.

The only game to be played by the School was netball, since there was no ground for any other; the School team had only moderate success in that first year, being beaten by Grey Coat and Streatham High, but defeating Surbiton High and the school next door in Elm House, run by Miss Blayney, who was soon to become yet another of the School's myriad friends. At the end of that first memorable term, a match was arranged between the best-looking girls in the School, and the cleverest, to be known as the "Beauty v. Brains" match; "Beauty" won, 8-7. Drill continued to be, as it had at Whitelands, an important feature of School life, and the Lady Margaret Drill Team came second in the annual competition held at Alexandra House Gymnasium. (Irene Lovett and Ruby Joselin were in both the winning drill team and the "Beauty" team.)

It is fascinating to follow up the careers of some of those pioneers of September 1917. For two at least, it was over almost before it had begun; the following April, little Nancy Yeo, aged 8, of Form I, died of meningitis (she was the daughter, incidentally, of a former Whitelands girl, and later College student, Florence Schott), and Gladys Munday, aged 16, of the Remove, was killed by the influenza that was sweeping the country at the end of the War. Mr Barnes's elder daughter, Winifred, went on to study at the London School of Economics; her younger sister Sheila became Head Girl in 1921, went on to St Andrew's University, and later trained as a teacher. Margaret Brice also became a teacher, as did many of MB's pupils, since she convinced them that her chosen profession was among the noblest in existence. Olive Barnard took up poultry farming, studied agriculture at Reading College, and eventually ran a farm in France. Ruth Elvy went into business on her own account, opening up a lingerie and dress-making concern, and advertising herself in the School Magazine. Olwen Jones became an actress, and Kathleen Clayton went into the Civil Service. Subsequent rather confusing exchanges of surnames indicate that several girls later married each other's brothers. Kathleen Beaumont read History at King's College, London, and Hazel Russell followed in MB's footsteps to Newnham College, Cambridge, and a lifetime's career as a teacher - a fitting tribute from her first Head Girl. Irene Lovett left in 1919 to work in the publicity department of Barker's of Kensington; while putting together a Christmas catalogue she engaged a young artist to illustrate it who was later to become very

Dorothy Eldridge, one of the original Fifth Form, 1917.

famous - Eric Fraser - whom she married in 1925. And little Pixie Ward, who had danced so charmingly before Princess Christian - she too grew up and trained as a teacher, ran her own dance classes as a hobby, and when war broke out in 1939 joined the Air Force.

All this had been achieved by the energy of a woman who would not take no for an answer, and who was determined that her girls should make the very best of themselves. The pupils of Lady Margaret were by and large drawn from the lower middle classes, their fathers being small businessmen, bank employees, insurance salesmen, and the like; their daughters had no great fortunes behind them, their intelligence and education were their major assets, and they had no illusions about the fact that they would need to earn a living when they left school. For those who ceased to improve themselves MB had nothing but scorn:

> *Our country needs the whole of all of us. You are only using a little bit of yourselves. You have presumably got sufficient brains and education to do skilled work, and you are not doing it. Of course we shall be beaten by the Germans after the war, if not in it, if we are satisfied in doing work that uses only a little bit of our intelligence, instead of training to do the very best we can....we have received so much that we ought to be ashamed of not contributing all we can...*   *(Magazine 1, 1917-18)*

Certainly there was much giving and receiving during those first two years. The School was running as a private school, and the money received in fees did not cover even the day-to-day expenses. The School was already heavily in debt, from the sum still outstanding from the purchase of the house, and this debt grew inexorably. The staff were grossly underpaid for all of this period, yet they soldiered on.

What undoubtedly saved the School during these difficult times was the army of well-wishers and supporters, and a few extraordinarily genorous benefactors, that MB gathered to her cause. They gave their time, their skills and energy, of course their prayers, and their money. Without them, and the drive of the woman behind them, the school at Parson's Green would have gone the way of others that tried to follow a similar course. Their names may reasonably fill a chapter in the history of Lady Margaret School.

Dramatis Personae

Enid Moberly Bell, Headmistress 1917-1947.

Enid Moberly Bell, the Founder and first Headmistress of Lady Margaret School, was born in Alexandria, in Egypt, on March 24th 1881; she was the daughter of Charles Moberly Bell, then the Egyptian correspondant of the Times. At the age of nine she was brought back to England when Arthur Fraser Walter enlisted his assistance in the management of the newspaper. She became a pupil of the Francis Holland School in Chelsea (the history of which she was later to write).

She grew up in a household through which passed a great many of the most distinguished, accomplished, and varied people of the day. Her father's position as managing director of one of the world's most influential newspapers made their house in Chelsea a veritable Mecca of the famous, talented, and well connected. The contacts made at this time were to serve her well in the future.

Enid was not satisfied, however, with the social round, no matter how fascinating, dazzling, and exciting it undoubtedly was. In her early twenties she went to India to teach, prompted by a missionary fervour that was part of her deeply held and lifelong Christian faith. The experience made her aware of her own academic shortcomings, and, anxious to further her studies, she returned to England in 1908 to take up a place at Newnham College, Cambridge, where at 27 she was something of a "mature student". In 1911 she achieved second class honours in the Classical Tripos; her father's death at the same time made it imperative for her to seek employment, and she obtained a post at Whitelands College School. Her doings thereafter have already been chronicled.

Throughout her life she was a passionate advocate for women, without in any way being a feminist in the modern sense of the word. She insisted that her girls were young ladies, and that they carried themselves well - to the last she considered deportment essential, and averred that you could always tell a Lady Margaret girl abroad in Fulham from the way she walked. But she insisted too upon high standards of scholarship and intellectual endeavour. She herself, among all the other commitments of a busy life, found time to write biographies of the women she admired - Flora Shaw, Octavia Hill, Josephine Butler - and a history of the struggle of women for recognition in the medical profession, aptly entitled *Storming the Citadel*. As the Times obituary put it, she had:

> ...a belief in the unique value of the individual founded on a deep religious faith...tireless energy, infectious enthusiasm and an almost ruthless determination to the tasks she set [herself].

Two other ladies deserve mention here, though their parts in this story will follow in due course. Edith Moberly Bell, MB's mother, was one of those women whom one suspects feminists must despise; born in 1854, she never held centre-stage, but her presence, support, and material assistance enabled first her husband to have the fulfilling career that he did, and then her daughter to perform her life's task of rescuing and establishing Lady Margaret School. (She lost both her sons in the Great War.) It was her stubborn persistence that obtained building clearance from the relevant Government department in 1917, and her Times shares that carried the School over its financial crises. She died on January 21st, 1933, and is commemorated by the carved Tablet outside the Headmistress's room.

Anne Lupton was born in Leeds, of a well-to-do family, and it was there that she began her life-long interest in "the housing question", that is, seeking to provide the homeless with somewhere decent to live. She came to London during the Great War to offer her voluntary services, but at first was rejected. Her health had always been a problem, and she had not taken her examinations at Cambridge, where she read Archaeology, for this reason. She became friends with MB, and for the rest of their lives they shared a house in Chelsea. This was her introduction to Lady Margaret School. After the War, she helped run the Fulham Housing Improvement Society, and a succession of Lady Margaret girls from the 1930s to the 1960s were privileged to help her in this work. Both she and MB had what is referred to as "ample private means"; with no need to work to support themselves, they were free to devote their time and energies to the welfare of others.

John Primatt Maud read History at Keble College, Oxford, and went on to Cuddeston College to study Theology. He was ordained in 1888, and served in a number of parishes, in London, Leeds, and Bristol. He had not long been a Canon of Bristol

Cathedral when he was consecrated Bishop of Kensington, on December 28th, 1911 (appropriately the Feast of the Holy Innocents), by the Archbishop of Canterbury. It was in this role that he entered the Lady Margaret story, as you have heard. The "St Paul's Review" said of him, when he died on March 21st, 1931:

> "A good man, skilled in the arts of speech" - all that and much more than that: "a forceful personality", as the Times described him in its obituary notice - that too, but more than that: a man of God, and a shepherd of souls; a lover of youth; impatient of shams of every kind; passionately devoted to the cause of righteousness, fair dealing and fair play; intolerant of compromise where vital principles were at stake, but human in every sense of a much abused word; wise in the council chamber with the wisdom which sees to the heart of issues and discerns the relative values of conflicting policies; in public presence, every inch a bishop, in private life, warm-hearted and genial; a good friend and, above all, a loving and devoted husband and father - such was John Kensington."
>
> (Magazine 15, 1931-32)

John Maud had served on a commission to the Bishop of Pretoria, and his interest in South Africa continued throughout his life. His daughter, as a memorial to him, helped organise a mission in that country, and for many years it received the support of the girls of Lady Margaret.

Edward Lyttelton was born on July 23rd 1855, into a very remarkable family. The first Baron Lyttelton had been a prominent statesman in the eighteenth century, and brother-in-law to William Pitt the Elder. Edward's father, the fourth Baron Lyttelton, a leading figure in the colonisation of New Zealand, had founded the city of Canterbury, the port of which was called Port Lyttelton after him. He had eight sons, of whom Edward was the seventh. Of those, one became a minister at the Colonial Office, another a bishop, a third a general, and Edward himself an extraordinary and influential educationist. His mother's sister was the wife of Mr Gladstone, the Prime Minister. In our own times, Oliver Lyttelton, 1st Viscount Chandos, was an eminent Colonial Secretary in the 1950s; and Humphrey Lyttelton, the jazz musician, is living proof of the versatility of talent in this particular family.

Edward Lyttelton was very much an athlete, but his great love was cricket. He was Captain of Cricket at Eton in 1874, and then of the astonishing Cambridge XI of 1878 that won every match it played, including one against the Australian team, when Lyttelton was the only man to make a century; he was perhaps the outstanding batsman of his day.

He was no slouch as a scholar either. He went up to Trinity College on a Foundation Scholarship, and in 1878 took second class honours in the Classical Tripos. He taught at Wellington for two years, and then returned to Eton in 1882 as a master. While he was there, he was ordained, and displayed yet another accomplishment, as a highly effective preacher. In 1890 he was appointed Master of Haileybury, and attracted sufficient notice that when Dr Warre, the Headmaster of Eton, retired in 1905, Lyttelton was appointed to succeed him.

He was by all accounts a much admired Head, and made a name for himself as a forward-looking, sensitive, and thoughtful teacher. He was not particularly interested in organisation and finance, but loved to deal with people and challenge their settled ways of thinking. A controversial sermon, delivered in March 1915, caused misunderstanding over his attitude towards the Germans, with whom we were at war; the accusation of pacificism hung over him, and he felt it necessary to resign the following year.

He was not one to waste time on regrets. He positively embraced his new-found freedom, finding time to think, to write, and to take up causes dear to his heart. It was at this stage of his career that Mr Barron, an Old Etonian himself, suggested his name to MB as a member of the Council she was forming to run her new school; he was then serving as a curate at St Martin-in-the-Fields. He accepted the offer with alacrity, and was appointed Chairman of the new body; as such he entered into the final negotiations with Whitelands over the future of the School.

He was within a few years to forge a closer link with Whitelands, for after the War, in 1920, he was appointed Dean of the College, where he served for the next nine years. In this new environment, known simply as "Doctor Ted", he was to be as influential and inspiring as he had been at Haileybury and Eton. He became a canon of Norwich in 1931, and did invaluable work in the diocese of Norwich. His last years were spent at Lincoln, where he died on January 26th, 1942.

He was, all things considered, a brilliant man. An inspired teacher, a first-rate sportsman, a sparkling preacher and speaker who could keep a table of people roaring with laughter throughout a meal with his humour and pungency, he was a remarkable catch for MB when she went a-trawling for friends to her new venture. He loved music and fresh air, he had a perennielly youthful temperament, and a shiningly saint-like character.

Sir George Robert Parkin was born in Canada on February 8th, 1846, the youngest of thirteen children of a farmer who had emigrated from Yorkshire. After attending his village school, he trained as a teacher, then spent three years at the University of New Brunswick. As soon as he graduated, in 1867, he was appointed Headmaster of the grammar school in Bathurst, and then in 1871 of the collegiate school at Fredricton, still only 25 years old.

In 1873 he came to Oxford, and in his year at Balliol was secretary to the Union Society, following a brilliant speech on the topic that was to become a passion with him, Imperial Federation - the notion that the British Empire should become one single, world-wide nation, not a collection of individual countries with a common allegiance. At Oxford he became friends with Alfred (later Lord) Milner, an influential member of the War Cabinet during the First World War, as was another friend from Balliol, Herbert Henry Asquith, later Prime Minister from 1908 to 1916. Another early friend was Edward Thring, the pioneering Headmaster of Haileybury; it was Parkin who, in 1898, wrote Thring's biography, as he had requested.

In 1874 he returned to Canada and resumed his Headmastership until 1889, when he took on the position of representative of the Imperial Federation League, travelling the Empire to spread the message; in the words of the Times, "he shifted the mind of England" on Imperial matters. In 1895 he was appointed Principal of Upper Canada College, Toronto, which in seven years he turned into the leading school in Canada.

He combined his two loves, education and Empire, when in 1902 he became Organising Secretary of the Rhodes Scholarship Trust, designed to unite through education the various peoples of the English-speaking world, and over the next few years he travelled extensively. In November 1916 he was in England to officiate at the Whitelands College School Prize-Giving, and therefore was no stranger to the School when MB enlisted his support some six months later. In the first year of Lady Margaret School, he was undertaking an important tour of the United States. He retired in 1920, and died two years later, on June 25th, 1922.

He was a tall, rather loose-limbed man, with enormous physical energy. He was all his life a convinced but broad-minded Anglican; he looked at every question from a moral, rather than a political, point of view. His position as a special correspondant of the Times made him known to MB, whose father was the Managing Director, and his services for the school were secured.

Sir Valentine Chirol - "traveller, journalist, and author", as the Dictionary of National Biography describes him - was not one of the original founders of the School, being in India at the time, but he soon after began so to interest himself in Lady Margaret that he was very quickly one of its most invaluable friends, and MB adopted him as an honorary founding father. He was born on May 28th, 1852, into a family of Huguenot extraction which had come to England following the revocation of the Edict of Nantes in 1685. His father was a Puseyite parson, who with his wife converted to Roman Catholicism some years before Valentine was born; and though he soon after reverted to the Church of England, his wife did not, and their son was raised in her faith.

Young Chirol was educated in France and Germany, and graduated from the Sorbonne. His experience was put to good use in the Foreign Office from 1872 to 1876. From 1876 to 1892 he travelled widely - the Near East, India, Persia, Australia. He was in Egypt and the Sudan during the Khartoum and Omdurman campaigns, acting as overseas correspondent of the London Standard.

In 1892 he became the Berlin correspondent of the Times - and so entered the magic circle where MB could find him many years later. Like Churchill in his "wilderness years", he wrote repeated early warnings of the growing threat of Germany to world peace, and consequently came into severe disfavour with the British Foreign Office; after the War, it was revealed that von Bulow, the German Foreign Minister (and later Chancellor), considered Chirol as one of the two Englishmen most dangerous to German interests.

From 1896 he was in charge of the foreign department of the Times, putting his considerable weight behind the Anglo-Japanese Alliance, the *Entente Cordiale* with France, the treaty with Russia, and the cause of permanent good relations with the United States - all of which policies became vitally important during the First World War. In 1908 he became a founding member of the newly formed Board of Times Newspapers.

His great and abiding love was India, and he was a leading influence on a number of bodies striving to introduce reforms into that country, including the Royal Commission on the Indian Public Services; for that he was knighted in 1912. He was in Paris for the Peace talks in 1919, playing a crucial role in keeping Britain and France in touch with one another.

Sir Valentine never married, perhaps because in such a busy life he never found the time. He was a water-colourist of some merit, if not distinction, and the School possesses a number of his paintings. He was from the moment MB recruited him a good friend of Lady Margaret; in 1919 he gave £1500 towards paying off the School's debts, and it was he who donated the two extra classrooms built at the end of what was the Hall, where the Gymnasium now stands; these rooms are now the gym changing room and showers. This was to be one of his last services to the School, for he died at his home in Chelsea on October 22nd, 1929.

The School in 1920.

MB and her Staff, c.1920.

Early days at Parson's Green

The Sixth Form, c.1920.

Despite all the difficulties, Lady Margaret survived its first year in fairly fine fettle. Numbers were increasing (159 in September 1918, and 205 in February 1920), enthusiasm and faith in a future for the School (despite a very daunting debt) were high, and the character and ethos of the place began to develop. It was not simply Whitelands transplanted; MB was not Miss Gregory. The beginning of the second year, in September 1918, saw the foundation of the Order. (The House system inherited from Whitelands, which used the term "order", had ceased to function, and the designation was there to be used for a new, and, as it turned out, longer lasting purpose.) Nowadays the Order is very much a prefectorial body, but at its inception it was clearly something else.

> *The Order of Lady Margaret School .... consists of girls who are considered efficient both in work and in general helpfulness; these girls help to manage a good many of the School affairs. Order meetings have been held every fortnight, at which School affairs have been discussed. New members are nominated and accepted by the Staff and the Order. The Order began with three Senior members and one Junior. There are now [September 1919] twenty-four members in the Senior branch, and five in the Junior.*
> *(Magazine 2, 1918-19)*

In short, the Order was an embryonic School Council. Pupil self-government was no new thing, of course, in the traditional and long-established boys' schools; but girls' schools in the early part of the century tended to be a great deal stuffier. This was an innovation, and was clearly only the start. In September 1919, Form Councils were set up, meeting once a week, which would deliberate and report to the newly formed School Parliament, which consisted of the existing Order and further delegates from forms otherwise not represented. The Head Girl, Hazel Russell, was Chairman, and Margaret Brice Secretary. The whole thing was managed in a very business-like way, and its first task was to review and revise the School rules, and add several new ones. Similar experiments were taking place just then in Moscow; it is, perhaps, a matter of regret that MB did not use the term "soviets" for her creations!

It was not all plain sailing for the new scheme. Within a year the Order abolished itself, because it considered the standards of its members too low! The Order was then re-established on a much more conservative model, with just six members. The Parliament continued as before, under the chairmanship of Evelyn Gooch, the new Head Girl, branching out into committees in true Westminster fashion.

At last, with the signing of the Armistice in November 1918, came peace. The whole school was assembled in the Hall for a short thanksgiving service. For the rest of the day, there were no thoughts of lessons. Instead, everyone was taken to Buckingham Palace, to see the parade of captured German guns, and to stand among the vast crowds outside the Palace to cheer the King and Queen when they appeared on the balcony.

> *I made the proposal impulsively to the school, and, of course, the children welcomed it with the wildest enthusiasm, and the staff, on whom, as always, fell the burden and heat of the day, responded as surely only a Lady Margaret staff would respond. Only Miss Ross mournfully suggested that she had better stay here with anything less than six years old.*
> *(Magazine 11, 1927-28)*

Somehow or other, everyone was got back safely to school, to experience one further delight - no homework that evening! The following July, a much smaller party, Miss Phillips, Miss Hartley, and the Order, stood outside St James' Palace to hear Peace finally proclaimed.

A very practical memorial to those who had died or been disabled in that conflict was the "Helping Hand" concert held in October 1918 to raise money to enable the daughters of such men to attend a school like Lady Margaret. This raised over a thousand pounds, and soon nine scholarships had been awarded.

Another mode of celebrating the peace that had now come to the world was the Pilgrimage of July 1919. MB (and her dog "Q"), Miss Phillips, Miss Hartley, and seventeen of the senior girls, walked the Pilgrims' Way from Otford (just outside Sevenoaks) to Chilham (then taking train into Canterbury itself). Irene Lovett (Mrs Fraser), sev-

The School Pilgrims at Canterbury, July 1919.

The School party at Lenham, July 1920.

Staff and Old Girls at Lenham (standing) Dorothy Eldridge, Miss Laughton, MB, Marjorie Clayton (on ground) Hazel Russell, Miss Phillips (with "Q").

The Kindergarten 1918. Miss Ross and Miss Sharp at the back.

enty-three years later, recalls the journey still as quite the most exciting time of her life till then, for she had never been on such a holiday before. Tramping through the countryside for five days, away from one's own family, sleeping fairly rough in strange houses, climbing hills and exploring ruins along the way - this was a liberated mode of living known to few girls at the time. MB had been compelled to open a new school, and she was determined that it would be like no other. Her polite, lower middle class girls took to the new freedoms with gusto.

> *None of us slept very much that first night at Wrotham. It was rather exciting sharing rooms and beds with people we had never shared with before. We were seventeen in one old cottage, and eight in one room. It was great fun, but not a very restful night.*
>
> *(Magazine 2, 1918-19)*

The third night was spent at Lenham, and clearly the school party made a good impression, for the following year the same three staff (and "Q"!) took twenty-nine senior girls there for a week of expeditions: the Old Palace at Charing, a fruit farm, Maidstone, Leeds Castle, Hythe - all were visited. They also worked on programmes of their own choice - architecture, local history, sketching, botany, literature - using the billiard room of a large house in the village as a schoolroom (when they were not working out-of-doors). On the Sunday, three recent Old Girls - Dorothy Eldridge, Margaret Clayton, and Hazel Russell (just about to go up to Cambridge) - joined them, looking very grown-up in their young women's clothes. During the same week, the rest of the senior school, in London, visited the Tower, the London Museum, and Hampton Court; the junior school had a party with games. The same thinking that was to develop Activities Week in the 1980s was already in evidence sixty-five years earlier; the elements of choice and adventure, valued even now for their educative merits, were then fairly wondrous innovations, and their place in the curriculum of the School from the earliest days gave Lady Margaret much of its special character.

The weekly War Lecture was another feature that added to the training and outlook of Lady Margaret girls in those early days. As a means of keeping her senior pupils in touch with what was going on in the world around them, MB required each member of the Fifth and Sixth Forms in turn to deliver a lecture to the assembled school on current events, as reported in the newspapers. This was not popular with the girls concerned, but undoubtedly helped to boost both their knowledge of affairs and their self-confidence.

Another venture was the Lady Margaret Club. Old Girls (including former Whitelands girls) could of course join the Old Girls' Association, and did. But something else was needed, a weekly rendezvous where friendships made at school between girls, and with the staff, could be continued and cemented in congenial and familiar surroundings. These were the days before radio and television, cinemas were in their infancy, and entertainment had to be largely home-made. The Club answered a need. Members would gather on a Friday evening to natter, drink tea, listen to talks, swap gossip, rehearse plays, and arrange dances and parties. They could even smoke, if they wished! On these occasions the staid members of staff could be seen in quite another light, especially Miss Phillips.

> *In more or less impromptu theatricals she is unequalled. During the last year we have seen her as a small boy in a sailor suit, Jack Tar hat well on the back of his head, firmly grasping his nurse with one hand, and a string ending in a toy dog with the other. Then she starred in "Scenes from Pickwick", as Mr Pickwick, and her representation of that worthy in night-shirt and night-cap proved too much for everybody's equilibrium. Her really perfect role to my mind though, was in the tableaux of well-known posters .... when at a moment's notice she appeared as "Oh, you dirty boy" (Pear's Soap) in knickers and a face smothered in mould from the Kindergarten tray.*
>
> *(Magazine 3, 1919-20)*

The ability of Lady Margaret staff to let their hair down on occasions is of course legendary. Hide-and-seek - with the staff hiding and the children seeking - was a very popular game at the Christmas Party.

> *After tea, all the lights were turned off except in the hall, and every Form had to find its Form Mistress in the dark. Great amusement was afforded in the search, especially when Miss Moberly Bell, who was hiding under a table, was mistaken for a trestle!*
>
> *(Magazine 3, 1919-20)*

The Pageant which had been staged for Princess Christian proved to be the first of a series of summer, open-air entertainments devised by the Staff and dressed mostly by Miss Laughton, involving large numbers of children of all ages, from the tiny tots in the Kindergarten to the revered mesdemoiselles of the Sixth Form. When the Princess again visited the School in June 1919, a "Fantasy", *The Piper of Dreams*, was devised to entertain her; Hazel Russell as the Piper invoked visions to a series of poets, from Chaucer to Tennyson, which were then acted out by the performers. In July 1923, a *Masque of the Seasons*, written by MB, was introduced by Father Time; Spring, Summer, Autumn, Winter, followed in due course, represented in poetry, singing, dancing, and display. In 1925 followed a *Pageant of London Town*, this time narrated by a Thames Nymph! She presented the personalities, sights, and sounds of the capital through its long history to the present day. 1927 saw a Nursery Rhyme Pageant performed by the Junior School, entitled *Mother Goose and her Goslings*, in which Pixie Ward, now grown up and left school, taught the music to the little ones. The 1929 production was entitled *The Pageant of the Gardens*; Betty Horner, the Spirit of the Garden, made the introductions, and by dancing, singing, and miming, the essence of the Garden was conveyed. Thereafter the themes were repeated, albeit to new audiences. *A Pageant of Parson's Green* was performed in 1932, and there followed in 1934 the *Pageant of the Seasons*, when it rained. In 1936 Father Thames guided the audience through another Pageant of London (*London Revisited*, as it was aptly called). This was to be the last of the pageants; the war intervened before another could be mounted, and since then they seem sadly to have become an unfashionable relic of a more graceful era.

"The Piper of Dreams", June 1919, Ruby Joselin as Jephtha's daughter "dressed in green and gold".

"The Piper of Dreams", June 1919. Hazel Russell in the centre.

"The Piper of Dreams", June 1919, Irene Lovett on left, Pixie Ward blowing the trumpet.

The Pageant of the Seasons 1934.

The Pageant of the Seasons 1934.

Problems

Meanwhile, the two ever-present problems, of space and money, continued to weigh on those with the School's interests at heart. Numbers were growing rapidly, and what had at first seemed perfectly adequate premises were becoming cramped and uncomfortable. (It was the story of Whitelands all over again.) The fees that the School felt able to charge its pupils hardly covered day-to-day expenses, despite the fact that the Staff worked for much less than reasonable salaries. At the beginning of its third year, the School was some two hundred strong; in order to make room for the last batch of admissions, the Remove had indeed already been "removed", to the end of next door's garden. Miss Blayney, the Headmistress of the little school then in Elm House (it was in fact a Home for delinquent girls!), kindly obliged with the loan of her kitchen for cookery classes (a Miss Shakespeare was engaged to teach the subject), and of a former laundry house which stood where the Geography Room now is, just as later she was regularly to oblige with the loan of her dining-room (what is now the Headmistress's room). The wash-house was far from ideal, especially in winter.

> *I am sure that those who learned or taught in that room have vivid and painful recollections of the hours spent there. We jumped for five minutes between lessons, we had runs round the garden on dry days, we piled on more and more clothes, but we remained bitterly cold.*
> *(Magazine 11, 1927-28)*

A new Hall was desperately needed. Hitherto the School had used Theodore Roussel's studio, but it was quite unable to house everyone at once. (As early as May 1918, the Council Minutes record a request by the Headmistress for "some sort of fan" to moderate the stifling atmosphere of this room when the whole school was assembled - and there were only 150 of them then!) Money would have to be borrowed to pay for the building, but the School's debt, despite Sir Valentine's £1500, and a generous donation from Mrs Carver, was still over £3000. The indefatigable Mr Barnes estimated the cost to be £2500, which would almost double what was owing. Two generous friends then stepped forward - Mr Wythes and Miss Lupton - and between them lent the money free of interest. (This loan was eventually repaid in full by 1926, after what seemed an endless round of money-raising events.) The Hall was built (where the gymnasium now stands) during the summer holiday of 1920, and for a while there was enough room again. The studio was converted into two classrooms, while Miss Blayney's laundry became the School's first chapel.

At the heart of the old Whitelands College stood the College chapel, used every day by the girls of the School. When the move was made to Parson's Green, the greatest sadness for MB and those who came with her was to leave this statement of faith and devotion behind. When the opportunity presented itself, to however inadequate a degree, to make good this loss, she took it, and on the School's third birthday, celebrated on Saturday September 25th, 1920, Bishop King of the Society for the Propagation of the Gospel (the Bishop of Kensington being ill at the time) came to dedicate it. Much work had gone into turning the drab building into something worthier.

> *We pulled down the laundry shelves, and an altar was made of their wood. We stained the floor, and colour-washed the walls, so that it is a very home-made concern, but one that is being increasingly beautified by many gifts and loans. (Magazine 4, 1920-21)*

(It was Miss Hartley's father, quite an elderly man by then,"who more than any other single person worked the transformation that made it into a Chapel", wrote MB later in her History of Lady Margaret School.) Over the years the little building was added to - furnishings, ornaments, stained glass - and became as much loved as its grander predecessor. It was lost, temporarily, in 1932, after Miss Blayney retired, but recovered when the School took over Elm House in 1938; it was then abandoned during the evacuation, but for twenty years after the Second World War it was the centre of the School's spiritual life. It was with a wrench that the School saw the end of it, in 1962, when the present Hall was built.

But a school cannot limp along from loan to sale of work for long. Some surer means of funding the School, without raising the fees beyond the ability of parents to pay, was needed; Bishop Maud sought desperately for such funds.

> *I will write to the National Society and see if it is possible to get a grant out of them. Whether the Diocesan Church Schools Association has any available funds I do not know, but I will find out. Whatever happens it would be suicidal as well as unchristian to starve the teaching staff.*
> *(Bishop Maud to MB, Oct 2nd, 1918)*

But to no avail. The School's peculiar position, and the manner of its founding, meant it did not qualify for such help. There were, it seems, just two options.

> *It seems clear that we shall have to adopt one of two alternatives, either come under the Board of Education and lose our independence, or keep quit of the Board and seek the protection of the "Schools Limited".* (Dr Lyttelton to Mrs Moberly Bell, Nov.26th, 1918)

("Schools Ltd." was an association of independent schools, which offered a modicum of protection and financial assistance to ventures such as Lady Margaret.) Eventually, at a Governors' Meeting on February 14th, 1919, it was decided to apply to the London County Council to become a Grant-Aided School. As a result of this decision, however, the Governing Body lost one of its founding members; Canon Carter, the Vicar of St Dionis', felt unable to come with the School in accepting the LCC grant, since it would in practice mean accepting some degree of public control; that, in his opinion, could jeopardise its position as a Church school, and he resigned. This was a sad blow, bearing in mind the crucial role played by Canon Carter and his wife in preserving the School two years previously. But the Governors felt they had no option, and went ahead with their application. Lady Margaret was inspected by the Board of Education, pronounced "efficient", and in 1921 was for the first time in receipt of some public funding. The annual deficits (nearly six hundred pounds in 1920, and well over a thousand in 1921) were turned thereafter into modest but regular surpluses. Under the new Articles of Government, there were to be six Representative Governors, chosen by the LCC, and twelve Co-optative Governors, that is, the former Foundation Governors. The new regime entailed rather more efficient book-keeping, and Mrs Moberly Bell, then Secretary to the Council, was appointed Clerk to the Governors, with charge of the accounts. This was a task she hated, having no great aptitude for accounts and figures, and in 1925 she gratefully handed the job over to the ever-faithful Miss Lupton, to whom the task was more congenial.

In the meantime, as the School awaited its possible grant from the LCC, an Appeal was launched in order to pay off the existing heavy debt. Bishop Maud wrote an impassioned prefatory letter to the appeal notice. He began with a brief summary of the founding of the School, then continued:

> *...From that day the school has gone forward with confident steps to its present flourishing condition both in numbers and tone.*
> *That it has so well succeeded is due in large measure to the self-sacrificing devotion of the staff, who have one and all worked at a rate of salary far below that which they might have secured elsewhere. With such teachers and leaders it is not surprising that a wonderful response from their pupils should be inspired, or that an atmosphere of enthusiasm for the highest ideals should pervade the School.*
> *As the parents whose children attend the school are people with small and fixed incomes, it is not possible to call upon them for increased fees...*
> *It is therefore to those who understand the vital issues at stake for the children of the Church at this momentous time that I venture to make an earnest appeal for support.*
> *It would be a tragedy indeed if such a venture of heroic faith were not assured of a worthy response from the body of Church people...* (Letter from Bishop Maud, July 1919)

Dr Lyttelton's fears that accepting public money would lay the School open to some degree of interference by the educational authorities, both local and national, were soon proved correct. The bureaucratic mind, as we have seen in our own times, does not always appreciate the peculiar nature, individuality and character of the institutions with which it sometimes has to deal. Instead, neatly drawn up plans, mulled over in some distant office far from the chalk-face and the living reality of schools as they are, fill its sight with enticing visions of administrative tidiness. To the LCC it seemed obvious that, with empty places in some of the surrounding elementary schools, and the need for more places in the secondary schools (especially for girls), the obvious thing for the new protege to do was to move its under-11s out and take in some more over-11s to fill the places. A conference was called by the LCC to discuss the age of admission to Aided secondary schools; Dr Lyttelton, unable to attend, made his feelings clear in a letter to Sir Valentine:

> *Parents who have regard to the importance of children being exposed to refining instead of coarsening influences cannot be expected to welcome the prospect of an elementary school for their children: things being as they are, that is a considerable proportion of elementary school children being brought up in homes marked by coarseness and neglect. To avoid this danger and being mostly indifferent as to the intellectual training they prefer to avail themselves of small shoddy private establishments, unrecognised and uninspected by any public body.*
> *Hence a good secondary school to which such children are sent later would find itself*

saddled with a large contingent of grossly ill-taught pupils who at 10 or 11 have to be taught the basest rudiments of how to learn.

(*Dr Lyttelton to Sir Valentine Chirol, Nov.28th, 1922*)

Those were the days when people chose not to mince their words! Dr Lyttelton batted on in fine style:

More grave even than the first objection is the violation of the one great foundation-principle which has been elaborated in England through the experience of many centuries: and was first discovered by the Jesuits, that everything depends in character-training on the first few years of human life....A school like Lady Margaret's does its permanent work by getting the children quite young and training them and the parents together in the great work of education for life. If the young children are withdrawn, nine-tenths of the power for good of our school will be lost: and that applies to the whole of the really efficient and effective secondary schools of London.

(*Dr Lyttelton to Sir Valentine Chirol, Nov.28th, 1922*)

The Church schools, as it turned out, were adamant that they would retain their junior departments, and the LCC were in no legal position to insist. The preparatory departments of Lady Margaret and similar schools across the capital in fact survived until the Education Act of 1944 put an end to them.

Thus for the moment Lady Margaret settled down to a comparatively trouble-free era, its problems of space and day-to-day finance overcome. There was, of course, still the original debt on the purchase of Belfield to be paid, as well as the loans from Mr Wythes and Miss Lupton, and periodic events - jumble sales, sales of work, and the like - were staged to try to meet these obligations. But for the rest of the 1920s, and the early 1930s, Lady Margaret could give its mind more or less entirely to the agreeable task of education in all its aspects.

A Form group, 1920.

The original Chapel at Lady Margaret.

Et In Arcadia Ego

With the building of the new Hall, serious drama became a possibility. It began auspiciously enough:

> On November 4th [1921], some of the seniors acted parts of ."Le Bourgeois Gentilhomme" under the direction of Miss Kirby. We made £17 for the Hall Fund. As Mary Hopper was ill at the last minute Miss Hobhouse most kindly played the part of M. Jourdain. We were very grateful for her timely aid.   (Magazine 5, 1921-22)

In 1923, the seniors presented another Moliere play, *Les Femmes Savantes*, and this time made £3.12s.9d. In March 1923, the Lady Margaret Club presented *The Knight of the Burning Pestle*, which MB directed and in which she played Pomponia; Miss Laughton, as ever, did the costumes. The following year the Club performed *Prunella*, by Laurence Housman and Granville Barker, and in 1925 *She Stoops to Conquer*. In 1927 they tried their hand at Shakespeare, with a production of *The Taming of the Shrew*, which Winifred Barnes directed; her brother was at the Royal Academy of Dramatic Art, and he and his student friends came in to coach the aspiring actresses. The main dramatic productions of the School itself were, of course, the periodic Pageants; but in 1927, for the 10th Birthday, Miss Phillips produced Laurance Housman's *Little Plays of St Francis*.

Another institution was the Ascension Day picnic, inspired by that pioneer effort at Whitelands in 1914. The first was held in 1919; after a eucharist at St John's Church, Walham Green, the entire School, except for the very little ones, made their way to the garden of "Ingarsby", Mrs Louisa Carver's house on the far side of Wimbledon Common. (The Carvers, it will be remembered, were cousins of the Moberly Bells.) The 1926 picnic was abandoned because of the General Strike, and later that year Mrs Carver's death meant that a particular era had come to an end. The outings continued, nevertheless, with a picnic and paper-chase on Wimbledon Common as the main attraction.

The 1919 Pilgrimage to Canterbury, and the 1920 expedition to Lenham, initiated a series of school trips of one kind or another. July, 1922, saw the first trip abroad, with a week in Paris. It was a mixed party: four mistresses (including MB and Miss Phillips) and 28 girls from Lady Margaret, Miss Richardson and nine girls from the Roan School, Greenwich, and three Old Girls - Olive Self, Hazel Russell, and Winifred Barnes. On Wednesday they visited the Louvre, and bumped into Miss Woodhouse and her mother. (Miss Woodhouse left Lady Margaret in 1925 to take up her appointment as Headmistress of Sidcup School.) The following evening they attended a performance of *Les Femmes Savantes* at the Comedie Francaise (no doubt the inspiration for the 1923 school production), and on Friday (Paris being crowded for the 14th) they visited Versailles and the Petit Trianon. The Empire Exhibition at Wembley drew four bus-loads of Lady Margaret girls determined to enjoy themselves; they spent six hours there looking at a very realistic display of *The Bombing of London* (grimly prophetic!), sheep-shearing from Australia, and an electrical relief map of the world in which Africa refused to work. A walking tour, in July 1926, was spent tramping from Devizes to Oxford, via Avebury, Marlborough, and the Ridgeway. In Oxford they visited several of the colleges before catching the train back to London.

Scenes from "Le Bourgeois Gentilhomme", November 1921.

The cast of "Prunella", February 1924.

Games, too, were flourishing. In 1923 new netball and tennis courts were laid, and the number of matches against visiting schools increased. At the end of that year, a new "house" system was introduced. (It will be remembered that the old system inherited from Whitelands had not survived the School's first year in its new home.) The School was divided into five "divisions", named after benefactors and founders of the School.

> An important change was made at the end of the Christmas Term, when the whole school was divided into games divisions. There are five of these, Kensington, Parkin, Chirol, Lyttelton and Carver. The tournament was held between divisions instead of forms. Carver won the first cup and Parkin the second.   (Magazine 7, 1923-4)

The Paris Trip, July 1922. At Versailles.

The new divisions not only competed in games. Each was made responsible for a section of the flower garden, and the Staff judged which had been best kept at the end of the term. Parkin division was to be short-lived; clearly, five divisions in a school the size of Lady Margaret were too many, and by 1925 the familiar present-day pattern was established.

The competitive spirit was inculcated early, it seems. The little ones in Upper Transition in 1926 wrote as follows:

On Ascension Day in the afternoon instead of having the usual lessons we had sports. We had three-legged races and all sorts of races. One of them was that we had to take off our shoes and go down to the other end of the Hall and come back and put them on again, and see who was first. One of the teachers mixed the shoes up so we could not pick them up strat away. It was such a muddle to get on our shoes after muddling them up. All the children that were eight or nine went together and they ran a race, and all the sevens and seven and a half. We had lots of fun. We rigalled throu the forms, and it was very funny to see us do it.

We had hopping along bars and jumping off them and running to the end of the Hall, and still there is something else to tell you. We had a three legid race and this was very exciting to the people falling over.

We had chocolate for prizes. The winner got a bar and the one that was second got half a bar, and we all got very hot doing all the things we had to do, and I liked it very much. I would have won the two legid race but I fell over with another girl called Rosie. And that's all I can tell you. Good-bye. (Magazine 9, 1925-6)

As to the raison d'etre of the School, a steady stream of girls sat their General Schools, Higher Schools, Matric, and Oxford Senior with varying degrees of success. Each year some proceeded to university and college, to study a variety of subjects. In one awful year, 1920, MB wrote tartly:

It is perhaps because we are so much occupied in all sorts of sorts of activities that we have done badly in examinations. All VI and Va took the London General Schools Examination and we did not gain any Certificate. This is an accident not to repeated, and the girls who failed and who are still in the School are going to pass the Senior Oxford at Christmas to prove that it was just a mistake. (Magazine 3, 1919-20)

The General School Certificate (the equivalent of later GCE "O" level and GCSE) was taken by most girls at the end of the Fifth Form; the examination was in a range of subjects, including English, mathematics, and French, and all had to be passed before a certificate could be awarded. The cleverest girls gained Matriculation, which was the necessary passport to the University; these normally stayed into the Sixth Form, while the rest left for work or further training of a vocational nature. The Sixth Form, therefore, by modern standards was very small, often no more than a dozen girls, and rarely exceeding twenty at Lady Margaret until the late 1940s. The girls in the Sixth Form then worked for their Higher School Certificates ("A" levels), before proceeding to their degree courses.

There were sad occasions too. In 1919, two girls, Constance Blades and Gladys Munday, died of the influenza then sweeping the country in the wake of the Great War, to be followed by little Irene Kennedy, aged 6, in 1921, Marjorie Horner, aged 13, and 7-year-old Marjorie Woods in 1922. Thereafter, the epidemic seems to have played itself out. On 25th June 1922, the School lost one of its earliest and most generous friends, Sir George Parkin, and the long Times obituary of this great man was reprinted in the School Magazine. A Memorial Fund was set up to provide books for girls going on to university, and Lady Parkin presented a framed photograph of her husband to the School. The following year, on 9th June, the School's Patron, the Princess Christian, died; she had presided, it will be recalled, at the new school's opening ceremonies. Her place as the School Patron was taken by her younger sister, the Princess Louise, Duchess of Argyll, who made her first visit to the school on July 3rd, 1924, in order to receive on its behalf the portrait by Mr Binney Gibbs of Dr Lyttelton which now hangs over the stairs in Lupton House. Mrs Carver, as we have recorded, died in 1926, on August 18th.

She was one of the earliest benefactors of the school and and only last October made another generous gift towards the reduction of the debt. But most of us knew her as our hostess on Ascension Day, where she invited all of us to her lovely garden on Wimbledon Common and let us have tea and play games all over it. She was a very old lady, but she always bore kindly with our noise. She used to come out onto the terrace to see us play, and she always asked Miss Bell to let us have a little longer when she began to talk about taking us home. We are all very grateful to her for all the pleasure she gave us.

(Magazine 9, 1925-26)

As the School approached its tenth Birthday, it seemed at last that the difficulties and problems it had experienced were things of the past. There were now some 250 girls in the School, the number originally projected at the School's foundation. At the meeting of the Governors on November 19th, 1926, the Headmistress announced that "A Parents' Association had been formed, of which the Governors were to be invited to be Vice-Presidents". The Association had in fact had its inaugural meeting the night before, and drafted a constitution. The Bishop of Kensington was to be President. One of the committee was Mr Cunningham, whose daughter Margaret, in the Upper Transition, was to go right through the School from five to eighteen, return as a teacher in the 1960s and 1970s, and finish up as Chairman of the Old Girls' Association.

In the autumn of 1926 also MB published her brief History of the School, recording for the benefit of present and past pupils, and for posterity, the epic story of the School's foundation, and its determined struggle to survive thereafter. She recalls the early days at Whitelands, the fateful day at St Dionis' Vicarage and the purchase of Belfield, the many friends and benefactors of the School. She ends with these words:

I have written this little account mainly because I want every Lady Margaret girl to know fully what she means when she says at Prayers every morning "I have a goodly heritage". Here is an account of your heritage. The School would not be here today if there had not been people willing and ready to give their prayers, their time, their energy and their money in order to make its existence possible. You must remember them all your lives with gratitude....   *(History 1926)*

As the School's tenth birthday approached, Miss Lupton, the new Clerk to the Governors, determined to do something about the huge debt which, despite sales of work and various generous donations, hung over the School.

Miss Lupton was horrified at the size of our debt, which amounted to nearly £3,600 when she took over the accounts, and decided that she couild not endure it. On November 1st, 1925, she attacked it, and by December 1st had collected £3,314, so that for the first time in our existence we were practically free from debt.   *(History 1926)*

When only £300 remained of the debt on the Hall, a donor stepped forward with "an anonymous gift sufficient to pay off not only the debt on the Hall, but also the original debt on the School building" (Magazine 10, 1926-7).

So the Tenth Birthday dawned, bright and fair. On Friday afternoon, September 30th, a Party was held, with a tea, charades, and a host of shared reminiscences. The following morning Bishop Maud celebrated the eucharist in the School Hall, and in the evening the Old Girls' dinner party rounded off the weekend. On the October 27th, a Speech Day was held, presided over by Bishop Maud, the Mayoress of Fulham, Mrs W J Waldron, MB, Sir Valentine Chirol, and Dr Lyttelton. The guest of honour was the Headmaster of Harrow School, Dr Norwood.

The Bishop opened the proceedings with a brief historical survey of the previous ten years, with much praise for "the splendid leadership of Miss Bell". The Headmistress followed, with an often rueful account of those early days, and thankfulness for what had been achieved. But she was determined not to rest.

We are now 252 children, of whom 44 are in the preparatory department. We have not built since 1919, but it may be that we have dreams. There are two which recur with increasing persistence. This hall is the only room we have which is not actually a class-room and full of desks. We must use it for assembly, for drill, for games on a wet day, and for dinner. We have no Art room. If we could have but two more class- rooms, the room behind us could become an Art room, which is after all what it ought to be, since before we invaded it, it was the studio of M. Theodore Roussel, who painted here his "Reading Girl", which has just been given to the nation. The other dream is of a real chapel.

(Magazine No.11, 1927-8)

All other debts now paid, a scheme dear to MB's heart, a Chapel Fund, had been launched, to raise the necessary capital to replace Miss Blayney's laundry with some-thing grander and more fitting. The proceeds from a performance of *The Little Plays of St Francis* had appropriately started the Fund off, and MB was able to announce, to applause, that she had "actually £5.5s. in cash towards it". Dr Norwood's address thereafter was almost an anticlimax.

No doubt as a result of MB's speech, the School received a particularly welcome tenth birthday gift. Sir Valentine Chirol, sitting on that platform and taking in what the Headmistress had said, generously presented the School with two new classrooms, in a wing built onto the hall. (The Chirol Wing still stands, though now converted to the gymnasium changing room and showers.) The two forms who were moved into them were the envy of the rest of the School.

> *They are lovely rooms, light and pretty with vivid blue paint, and with windows through which you can rather distractingly see the garden growing.*
>
> *(Magazine 12, 1928-9)*

They were, in fact, the first purpose built class-rooms in the School's history. Furthermore, with the fulfilment of one of MB's dreams, the other became possible, and Theodore Roussel's old studio became the Art Room that she had wished.

And so, ten years old, with its desire for money and space temporarily satisfied, Lady Margaret School could face the future in fine spirits. Those future years would be largely good ones, but, true to form, they would be anything but restful.

The Sixth Form, c.1924.

A Form group, c.1924. The teacher is Miss Winchester.

38

An uneventful
sort of life

So we settled down to an uneventful sort of life, and most people barely noticed the changes that were taking place.
(History, 2nd ed 1938)

So wrote MB of the years following the tenth birthday. Perhaps she had other things in mind when she referred to "changes", for changes certainly did occur. For one thing, there were farewells to be said as the School lost first one, then another, of its original friends.

Sir Valentine Chirol was at the official opening of the two classrooms that bore his name; they were to be his last gift to the School, for he died the following year, in October 1929, aged 78, at his home in Chelsea. He had been a life-long friend of MB's family, and she recalled:

> *I do not know when I first saw him, I think it was probably before I could speak. I do not really remember him until we came to live in London, which happened when I was nine years old. He used to come to our house a great deal when I was a school-girl and we all loved his visits. He had travelled so much, he had been to every capital in Europe except Monte Negro, and that made him an exciting person to us. He used to take us out "on the spree", and he always had interesting things to tell us. He could sing, he could sketch, and he had all sorts of queer and beautiful things to show us in his flat. I remember one Christmas he and my Mother wrote a play about China for us to act, and I was the Empress of China, and he gave me that beautiful Chinese robe to wear, which now always appears on one of the Kings in our Nativity Tableaux. (Magazine 13, 1929-30)*

He had in the twelve years that he was associated with Lady Margaret been extraordinarily generous of his time, money, and support. He has two surviving memorials in the school: the portrait by Sir John Collier, which hangs alongside that of Dr Lyttelton over the stairs in Lupton House, and Chirol division that was named after him. He also presented the School with a grand piano, which was sold in the 1960s and the money used to buy the two John Pipers that now hang outside the Chapel; so in a sense, they are his memorial too.

Earlier, in March 1929, Miss Blayney, of Elm House next door, retired; her successor was a Miss Ball. Her first action was rather high-handedly to withdraw two of her girls from Lady Margaret before they had finished their secondary education; it was not clear whether the Managers of Elm House had authorised this move, which boded ill for the spirit of cooperation between the two establishments that had existed so long. Miss Ball continued to make part of her garden available, but no longer could spare the dining-room; what was worse, in 1932, the School lost the use of the chapel building, and a prefabricated shed at the end of Belfield's garden had to be used in its place.

In 1930 the Thumwoods retired. They had come to the school soon after its opening, Mr Thumwood as schoolkeeper, and his wife as housekeeper. Mr Thumwood had been MB's grandfather's gardener when she was a child, and he and Mrs Thumwood, already past pensionable age, were very eager to help when the School opened.

> *They belonged to a generation which was passing away even when I was young. She always "bobbed" to me when I spoke to her, while he touched his forehead, since his head was bare.*
> *(History, 4th ed 1967)*

They were replaced by Mr and Mrs Edwards, who were to continue serving until Mr Edwards's sudden death in 1961.

Then, in March 1931, the School lost its founding father, the Bishop of Kensington - "John our Bishop", as he was affectionately known. MB wrote:

> *The loss to us is indeed a heavy one. We are blessed with many benefactors and friends at Lady Margaret School, but John our Bishop must always come first in our memory, for indeed the School would not be here but for his faith and courage. And having made its existence possible, he never for a moment lost interest in it. He came to our Birthdays, he came on Ash Wednesday, he quite often came to Governors' Meetings - always when there was any special problem to be solved. He was ready with encouragement and with advice, with practical help for the School or for any individual. Nothing was too small for his consideration, nothing that touched anyone of us unimportant to him. The best thing of all to remember is that he really loved the School and enjoyed coming to us.*
> *(Magazine 15, 1931-32)*

Many of the School attended John Maud's memorial service at Christ Church, Lancaster Gate, on March 23rd, and then his funeral in St Paul's Cathedral. A service of Holy Communion was held at the school a week later in his memory. Two permanent memorials to the Bishop remain: Kensington division itself, and the institution of Foundation Day, on March 18th, the day when, in 1917, Bishop Maud and MB had first seen the way to saving the School.

> *The Head Mistress also reported that the children themselves had asked that they might have an annual service of commemoration in March, at the anniversary of the School's foundation. This was unanimously approved.* (Minutes, Nov.11th, 1932)

In January 1933, Mrs Moberly Bell died. Ethel Moberly Bell had from its beginning been a staunch supporter of the School that her daughter had rescued from the ashes of Chelsea; it was she who had badgered the Ministry of Munitions for the priority certificate that enabled the work to be done on Belfield House before the School could move into it. She did more than that:

> *Money was the first need, and at once Mrs Moberly Bell, who was one of those at the heart of the enterprise, deposited her Times shares at the bank to guarantee the necessary overdraft. These shares represented her main source of income, but, more than that, they were her dearest possession, for they had been given to her by the Company after her husband's death in harness.* (Notes by EMB for 50th Anniversary)

It was these shares that carried the School through from one financial crisis after another in its early days. It was she who had gathered many of her personal and family friends to form the first Governing Body, and then had been its first Secretary, and later Clerk. The portrait of this woman that emerges from MB's biography of her father is a memorable one:

> *If you have read it, you will have got an impression of her able, witty, charming personality, her eagerness in seizing every opportunity for hospitality and friendship, and her capacity for smoothing the ways of her brilliant and hard- worked husband, for whom she made the perfect complement.* (Magazine 14, 1932-33)

The Governors took the unprecedented step of granting MB a week's extra holiday, to be taken when she felt the need of it, as their acknowledgement of the grief she clearly felt. A more permanent memorial was the wooden tablet, inscribed with the names of the three Foundation Governors - Mrs Bell, Sir Valentine, and Bishop John - which now hangs in the entrance hall of Lupton House, outside the Headmistress's room. It was carved by Mr Harry Parr, an artist, and a parent of children in the School.

Dr Lyttelton's appointment to a post out of London meant that he could henceforth only rarely attend Governors' meetings; and although he did not resign, he ceased to be the familiar figure about the School that he had hitherto been; his name (frequently misspelt!) lives on in the Lyttelton division. Mr Wythes, too, because of the increased pressure of his work as a magistrate, felt it necessary to resign, in February 1935, and the School lost another very generous benefactor. Earlier, in March 1934, the Hon. Miss Mary Pickford died; she had been on the Governing Body since the beginning, and had worked assiduously for its well-being. She had been elected MP for North Hammersmith in 1931, and had been appointed the only woman member of the Joint Select Committee on Indian Reform. Her place on the Governing Body was taken by her sister Dorothy.

Meanwhile, the School proceeded with its work. At the end of 1929 there was an inspection by the Board of Education. Their report began with glowing praise for MB.

> *Before the entrance of the Head Mistress, Miss Shearson said the Inspectors had formed a very high opinion of the character and personality of the Head Mistress, who knew the School and everyone in it, was not ignorant of its weaknesses and was keenly interested in every side of its work.* (Minutes, Nov.15th, 1929)

The School had been given a thorough inspection, and the buildings were pronounced sufficient to accomodate the pupils, if not fully satisfactory or convenient. There was a need for an extra playing field, the Hall had to be used for too many different purposes, the laboratory was too small, more blackboards were needed, and a specialist Geography Room should be created. The Inspectors recommended that the School adopt "a formal agreement with parents to leave their girls for the full secondary course, in place of the tacit understanding that exists at present".

There were hopes of new building, even an offer from the LCC to build a new dining room, so that at least one of the Hall's many functions could be moved elsewhere. But the country's economy was now in recession, with the financial crisis of 1931, and all improvements had to be abandoned for the moment. The LCC even approached the

Governors to increase the school fees, as a means of raising extra cash, and so relieve the public purse; the Governors at first refused, as many parents were already finding the present level of fees difficult to meet, but eventually agreed to raise them to £4.10s a term. Another economy that was implemented was to cut the schoolkeeper's wages by 2 per cent, to bring him into line with his colleagues in other schools!

The financial crisis of 1931 was the first cause of the drop in the number of children in the Kindergarten. Fulham, too, was changing, with families with young children moving to the new estates further out of London. By 1934, the Preparatory Department, which at one time had nearly 80 children in it, numbered just over 30.

The tennis team, 1934.

The long illness of Miss Ross, her death in 1934, and the departure soon after of her successor Miss Kent, did nothing to help matters. Cicely Ross had come to the School at the end of its first year; it was she who had modified Miss Bell's madcap scheme to take the whole School to Buckingham Palace on Armistice Day, and insisted on remaining behind with the youngest children.

> *The children felt safe and comfortable with her, she was always the same. When she said a thing she meant it, what she meant one week she meant the next week. She took it for granted that they were reasonable beings, she had no "baby talk" for them. They were not "kiddies" or "little ones", or any of these things, just individuals whom she expected to behave reasonably at the stage they had reached. They gained confidence because they knew just what she expected of them. As they grew older and passed into the main school they began to realise her more as a person, and to appreciate her steady interest in them.*
> *(Magazine 15, 1933-34)*

As a practical step towards stemming the alarming drop in numbers in the Preparatory Department, MB bought a car to use as a school bus for the smaller children. And in order to remain attractive to both sexes at Kindergarten age, the Governors in 1938 decided to engage "a young man to teach the small boys football". (Minutes, Oct.28th, 1938)

At the same time, the numbers in the senior part of the School were increasing, so much so that the Sixth Form had to move out of the little room on the first floor which it had occupied from the beginning, and move into the Art Room, M. Roussel's old studio.

The customary round of school life continued. Matches were won and lost, girls were prepared for confirmation, which took place annually in the School Chapel, plays were rehearsed and performed - *A Midsummer Night's Dream* in 1930, Masefield's *Tale of Troy* in 1933, with the Lady Margaret Club presenting Gordon Bottomley's *Gruach*, a musical version of *Macbeth*, in 1931. A Dramatic Society was formed in 1934, to read and discuss plays. There were the ongoing Pageants, in years when there was not a play.

A junior school Form group, c.1930.

The end of the Summer Term developed into School Journey Week, very much like the present-day Activities Week, except that it happened only every other year. In 1933 there was an expedition to Cornwall, which included an exciting visit to Tintagel. For the "stay-at-homes" there was The Week in London, during which the girls visited the Royal Mint, Southwark Cathedral and the George Inn, Covent Garden, and the Inns of Court; the grand climax on the Friday was a country walk through Chorley Woods, where the juniors found somewhere to paddle. Two years later, there was a trip abroad, to Bruges, while the London Week pupils went to Box Hill and - Covent Garden! By 1937 the planning was growing more elaborate and adventurous; there were two residential trips: twenty girls went to the Isle of Wight, and thirty to Switzerland, while the Londoners revisited Box Hill and the Law Courts, and took a boat down-river to Greenwich.

The big event of 1937, of course, was the Coronation of King George VI and Queen Elizabeth (now the Queen Mother). The LCC made arrangements for representative parties from all the London schools to occupy a place along the route of the procession, and Lady Margaret supplied its quota of patriotic cheerers and wavers.

Margaret Cunningham, later to be a member of the Staff, was a girl at the School during this period. When she retired in 1976, she penned these memories for the Magazine:

THE LIFE AND CRIMES OF MARGARET CUNNINGHAM AT SCHOOL
First you must imagine the age range: 5-18, not 11-18. One form of each age, not two. I started at Lady Margaret School, aged 5, in the Kindergareten. After that there was Lower Transition, Upper Transition, First Form (ages 8-9), II Form, III B, III A (ages 11-12), IV B, IV A (= the present III Form), V B, V A, VI Form (ages 16-18) - thirteen years from top to bottom. Nowadays it would be very unusual to attend one school for thirteen years.

Lady Margaret girls at the Coronation, May 1937.

We wore navy blue tunics with box pleats, typical of the day. Not pretty in any case, and positively ugly if you were fat (which I was not). In winter we wore this under our butcher blue overall with a black bow, decorated with our House colour. We also wore Ward shoes and sling purses, which did away with some noise and lost money. I can't think why these two blessings were ever abolished.

Crimes I can remember.

1. Aged about seven or eight. Had been wasting time. Punishment to sit in Entrance Hall and watch the clock for one whole hour, where Miss Kent (the Secretary) and many other important people could see me and how silly I was.

2. Aged about eleven. Mark of 0% for needlework, which indicated that I hadn't been trying. In class I was usually reading aloud to the class so of course I hadn't the faintest idea what a "run and fell" seam was; I don't even now.

3. Same age. Didn't buy dinner ticket in morning but slunk out (with friends) to Lyons at Walham Green (now Fulham Broadway) to buy steak and kidney pudding, which was much nicer and cheaper than school dinner (a shilling). This was found out, because I had told one of the Order, not realising that she would split. Actually, I think the Headmistress thought I had been rather clever, but she pretended to be cross.

4. In Form IV A. In prep a gang of us noticed a barrel-organ man outside our form-room (now the Biology Lab), so we gave him a few pennies to come back during Scripture. This, rather to our surprise, he did. This reduced considerably the boredom of the Epistle to the Ephesians, and was never found out.

5. In the VI Form and quite old enough to know better. Talking at the top of my voice in the library. Caught by Headmistress. Was sent down to join V B for Maths. This hurt, because (a) V B's Maths was very boring and much too easy for me; and (b) Miss Winchester, who treated me as an equal most of the time, was teaching it. Also (c) V B, which contained a few young friends of mine, could observe the disgrace.

We learnt a great deal by heart, because the Headmistress said that what you learnt when young stayed in your head, and what was learnt when older did not. How right she was! I am really grateful for all this hard work. French, English, even Latin, I can still remember clearly, and large chunks of the Bible. We had to learn a verse a day, and on Fridays had to chant all five learnt in the week in unison. On the penultimate day of every term, there was "repetition" in Hall, from which the very young were excluded; this was preceded by the writing out of the Scripture verses. Marks were "perfect", "not perfect", and "returned". I was quite good at this and don't remember any returned work of this kind. Results were read out, eg III A, two perfect, twelve not perfect, six returned.

Pageants we had, produced with infinite patience by the Head. These involved individuals of all ages, choirs, original songs. When very young I think I was Curlylocks or Mary Mary or some such. Nativity tableaux alternated with performances of parts of Handel's Messiah. School plays and drama competitions between houses took an honoured place. I was Antonio in the Trial scene from "The Merchant of Venice" in my last year when I was captain of Lyttelton.

We seemed to have time for everything but academic work. Even so, two of us managed to enter Universities well before we were 18. When we left school the Headmistress said, "Marjorie and Margaret almost came to the school in their perambulators." Great fun it was.
(Magazine 1975-76)

Margaret Cunningham in the Kindergarten (she is the girl sitting far right; the little boy in front of her is her brother).

Naboth's Vineyard

We had always wanted Elm House. When Miss Blayney resigned there was some question of her school being given up and our taking it, but that, as you know, did not happen. When we simply had to have more space, we naturally turned our eyes in this direction again.
(History 2nd ed 1938)

The School in 1935. "Naboth's Vineyard" - Elm House - next door.

In an earlier chapter, we traced the history of Hore's (or Parlor's) tenement as far as the 17th century, when the stories of Belfield and Elm Houses took their separate ways. Sir Francis Child had let the tenement to Ralph Grange; on his death it was purchased by Charles Chambrelain, who himself died on January 29th, 1704/5. Chambrelain left what was to be the Belfield part of the estate to his married daughter Abigail, wife of Lemyng Rebow. The other part eventually (in 1724) went to Chambrelain's granddaughter Rachel, married to John Gerard de Hopman. In 1729 the de Hopmans advertised the house to let, in The Country Journal for 5th July. It becomes clear why, at around this period, it acquired the name of Elm House.

On Parson's-Green, near Fulham, Middlesex, To be Lett a large convenient House, with an Orchard, well-planted Gardens, Stable, Coach-Houses, and Out-Houses, a Row of large Elms before the Gates, pleasantly situated on a very healthy Ground. The House is fit for either Courtier, Merchant, or large Boarding-School. Enquire at the House near the White House on Parson's-Green, on Mondays, Wednesdays, and Fridays.

(The White House occupied the site of Henniker House, acquired by the School in the early 1950s)

After several further lettings, the house was taken by the Rev. William Pearson in 1803, who used it as a school for boys until 1811; in 1809 he published a small text-book entitled "Short Speeches, selected for the use of Young Gentlemen of the Seminary at Parson's Green, Fulham". From 1811 to 1832 Elm House was conducted as a Roman Catholic school by a succession of gentlemen: Francis Quequet (till 1814), Henry Daniel (till 1822), Owen Morrice (till 1826), and his son the Rev. Richard Morrice (till 1832). Two military gentlemen, Lt-Col. J N Abdy and Major-Gen. Sir Joshua Webb, lived there in succession in the middle of the century. In 1890, having stood empty for some time, it was converted into a Roman Catholic School of Discipline for Girls. This was later to become Elm House School (or "Miss Blayney's School", as it was known to its neighbour in Belfield), run under the auspices of the Home Office as an Approved School, where girls in need of sympathetic, but secure, oversight might be housed.

In May 1935 Lady Margaret was inspected by the LCC.

... the inspectors said we could not really do ourselves justice in our crowded quarters. They say we can hardly go on without a Library, a Lab. twice the size of the present one, a Dining Room separate from the Hall, an Art Room not used as a class-room. (There are other things they would like us to have, but these they consider indispensible.) We do not know how we shall set about all this but we shall certainly have to pull down the Art Room and build a two-storey block there, and perhaps do the same with the Hall.
(Magazine 17, 1934-35)

Plans for these developments were actually drawn up, but it was clear even from these that more than ingenuity would be needed to get the Lady Margaret gallon into the Belfield pint pot. The house and its grounds clearly would no longer "do". There was talk of moving the school out of Fulham to some more spacious suburb, or of its closing altogether. It was the Whitelands saga all over again, but worse, since so much effort and affection had gone into this venture, which now was very much the victim of its own success.

Elm House next door was having similar problems of overcrowding, and it was mooted that the school there might seek larger premises elsewhere. Immediately tentative negotiations were put in train, a letter being sent to the Managers of Elm House, so that Lady Margaret might move sideways in its quest for more space. There followed a frustrating delay, while the LCC dragged its feet on the matter, but finally, on July 3rd, 1936, a small sub-committee was set up, consisting of Miss Holman, Miss Duff, and Miss Lupton, to begin what was to prove an arduous and lengthy marathon. Elm House had apparently found some suitable alternative premises, and had set in motion the process of buying them. Anne Lupton, in over-confident anticipation of the outcome, was already planning the removal of the wall between the two gardens (letter July 5th). Audrey Duff, meanwhile, was looking into the legalistic details; the original Trust Deed covered only Belfield specifically, and a new arrangement would have to be

The garden, behind Belfield. Over the wall, Elm House. 1935.

made to cover Elm House (letter July 9th). (Audrey Duff had been recruited to the Governing Body by MB and Miss Lupton; she was very active in the Family Welfare Association. She remained a Governor and friend of the School until her death in September, 1974.)

Unfortunately, the Elm House trustees had realised that they had Lady Margaret School over a barrel, as the saying goes. Mr Vyvyan Hicks was handling the matter for Elm House, and was clearly an astute worker; furthermore, time was on his side rather than the other way about. Lipton and Jefferies, representing Lady Margaret, were quite frank in their reply to Miss Lupton, whose anxieties increased as the year moved on.

> *I quite understand your difficulty in this matter, but as it is apparent that possession cannot be obtained in any event until December, I am inclined to the view that it is worth the risk delaying any further approach to the other side. It is apparent your keenness to buy is causing the price to be inflated.   (Letter to Miss Lupton, Aug.7th, 1936)*

A personal approach was tried, through individual members of the committee of Elm House, but at that juncture they had to withdraw their offer for new premises they had found because of restrictions as to their use placed upon them by the vendors. Mr Hicks did not hestitate to take advantage of the new delay.

> *You will readily understand that my clients must not be left without a satisfactory house for the children at Elm House and they do not know of one at present. Subject to what I have written above, if your clients are desirous of making an amended offer, it could be placed before the managers at the end of this month...*
> *(Letter to Messrs Lipton and Jefferies, Sept.3rd, 1936)*

So matters remained, until the energetic Miss Lupton decided to take matters into her own hands. She began searching for a property that would answer all the Elm House requirements. At her instigation, a survey was made of The Chestnuts, on Putney Hill, on December 17th. With nearly an acre of ground, three large reception rooms, and some fifteen bedrooms, it seemed ideal; but it did not apparently suit Elm House's purpose. Another house, by Wimbledon Common, was found, and rejected.

Then, early in the new year, Miss Lupton received details of "Bryntirion", 104 West Hill, in Putney. It was some £1500 dearer than The Chestnuts, but promised to be something that Elm House could not reasonably refuse. And so it turned out.

104 West Hill, in 1992.

> *I am informed that the Home Office and the Managers have approved of the house No.104 West Hill, East Putney, and I am expecting a reply from the owner's solicitors informing me whether there are any covenants, restrictions, stipulations, or any other thing which would prevent the full use of the premises for the purpose for which they would be required if bought.   (Letter from Mr Hicks to Miss Lupton, Feb.9th, 1937)*

Mr Hicks's next letter (Feb. 16th), however, contained a demand from the his clients for not less than £5000 for Elm House; Miss Lupton had originally offered £4000. The LCC were quite unwilling to assist in the purchase of the house at what they thought a very inflated price. Miss Lupton felt obliged to turn down the suggestion of £5000, while hinting that her original offer might be increased. Mr Hicks's reply was brief:

> *Thank you for your letter of the 24th ult. In reply to the last paragraph, my clients cannot arrange for the purchase of the new property until they know whether Lady Margaret School is willing to pay the price wanted for Elm House.*
> *(Letter to Lipton and Jefferies, March 1st, 1937)*

Elm House held all the cards, and Miss Lupton, with as good a grace as she could manage in the circumstances, agreed to meet their demands. Then, just as everything seemed to be coming to a resolution, fate landed a body blow that would have felled a giant. Mr Hicks again:

> *Thank you for your letter of the 11th inst., on receipt of which my clients made an offer to buy the house of which I wrote to you. I regret that my clients were then informed that it had already been sold; and they are now going to build on their own property.*
> *(Letter to Lipton and Jefferies, March 16th, 1937)*

It seemed that all the strenuous efforts of the past six months had been in vain. But that was to reckon without Anne Lupton! Like the great Alexander before her, when faced with the Gordian knot, she seized her sword, or rather, the contents of her bank account and her shares in the Bwana M'Kubwa Copper Mines, and within two weeks had redeemed the property from those who had just bought it; then, lest her resolution cool, she offered it to Elm House, they accepted, and the thing was done. The Elm House children were to move to West Hill, and Elm House and a thousand pounds were to be handed over to Lady Margaret. There was still the question of whether the Putney house could be used for its new purposes, and at first this was refused; Miss Lupton would have a useless building left on her hands. But she had the bit between her teeth now, and her representations to the Planning Authorities had the decision reversed (letter April 5th). The Education Officer at County Hall was triumphantly informed that Lady Margaret could now go ahead with the required improvements. On April 30th, Lipton and Jefferies announced what they optimistically thought was the completion of the purchase, at well over £6000; Elm House had been a costly venture, but with it the School's survival was assured.

But everyone had reckoned without the redoutable Mr Hicks. He suddenly announced that he was unwilling to sign the final settlement until an amendment had been made to it that would have made Miss Lupton responsible for all necessary works that his clients might have to carry out at West Hill to adapt it to its new purpose. He ignored a whole string of letters sent him by the Governors of Lady Margaret, and finally, on May 27th, they wrote in the strongest terms direct to the Managers of Elm House.

> *In the Draft Contract sent to Mr Hicks, in which we agree to pay "reasonable and proper" legal costs and expenses, Mr Hicks deletes the words "reasonable and proper". This displays a frame of mind in keeping with his conduct of this case, but hardly in accordance with the best traditions of his profession.*
>
> *My Governors feel bound to protest very strongly against being treated in this manner: against the deletion of these words in the Contract; and against being involved in charges which your solicitor himself is unwilling to limit by the qualifications "reasonable and proper".* (Letter from A W D Reid to Elm House Cttee, May 27th, 1937)

Meanwhile, Miss Lupton met those costs which considered "reasonable and proper", including the drains and electrical installations. The LCC, too, were working towards an agreement as to how much rent should be paid to Miss Lupton for Elm House, since she was technically its owner; a sum of £250 a year was fixed upon. On August 12th, Lipton and Jefferies were able to report:

> *With regard to the legal arrangements for completion, these are perfectly satisfactory, and you will no doubt be pleased to know that Mr Hicks has gone away to recover from his nervous breakdown. However, as far as we are concerned here we see no reason why the matter should not be completed on the 10th September, provided Mr Hicks does not prolong his holiday.* (Letter to Miss Lupton, Aug.12th, 1937)

The Isle of Wight, July 1937.

In that pious hope, Mr Jefferies was to be proved wrong. A protracted wrangle over Mr Hicks's costs, which he insisted Miss Lupton pay, then ensued, and was not finally settled until February 1938! However, the transfer of Elm House to Lady Margaret School was at last completed on October 29th, 1937; the thing was signed and sealed, Anne Lupton could now draw breath, and MB had her Naboth's vineyard.

Switzerland, 1937.

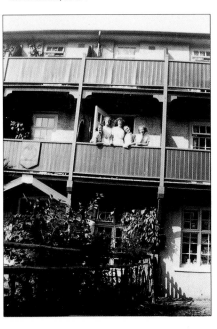

45

Coming of age

"Naboth's Vineyard". Elm House in 1938 undergoing alterations.

The gardens in 1938: looking down on the new Chapel.

The new Chapel 1938.

The occupants of Elm House moved out on September 7th, 1937, and it was agreed that Lady Margaret could begin moving in straight away. But the place looked like a wreck, as a newly vacated house will, and workmen had hurriedly to make it presentable in the week that remained before the beginning of term. This miracle was accomplished, the building was blessed by the senior curate of All Saints', Fulham, the Rev.M McLeod, with prayers in every room, and then the school began to move in.

The first change was in the name of the building. Had it not been for Anne Lupton, Elm House would not have been the School's to occupy and enjoy; indeed, the School might well have found it impossible to continue at all. Her timely intervention and initiative, and her generous outpouring of money, had saved the day, and in recognition of this the new building was renamed Lupton House in her honour.

MB was the first to benefit from the new order; she had a new and larger room to go to (what is now the upper Staff Room), and a procession of girls carried her books across to her new premises. (It would be another year before the two houses were connected; meanwhile, everyone had to go out of one and into the other!) The Sixth Form, now numbering eighteen, had for some time needed a room large enough to hold them all, and they received the balcony room on the top floor (what is now the Sixth Form Art Room); the Order had an additional room next door.

The acquisition of Elm House meant that Miss Blayney's old laundry building, that had for years been the School Chapel, could once more be used for this purpose, and on the School Birthday the Bishop of Kensington rededicated the building to this sacred use. But it was clear that it was not very convenient for the growing school; it was cramped and so damp that the vestments had to be hung out to dry before every service. Then an old friend of Miss Phillips visited the School, saw the chapel, and offered to pay for its rebuilding as a Christmas present to mark that eventful year. The work was done immediately, and the new Chapel was dedicated on the School Birthday of 1938. The two windows behind the altar were filled with stained glass by Miss Howson, one-time Mayoress of Fulham as well as an accomplished artist; these again were paid for by generous benefactors, and depicted the Lady Margaret Tudor and Bishop John Maud.

Then, in March 1938, the old Kindergarten room, along with the whole of the end of Belfield adjoining Lupton, was demolished, in order that the archway and classrooms which now connect the two houses could be built. As this proceeded, lessons continued to be taught, interrupted continually by

> .... *deep digging and hammering, and showers of dust and dirt, and brickbats rattling down the chimneys and holes appearing in the corners of rooms. The Staff learned to teach louder than the builders hammered, and to continue unperturbed when a cloud of dust suddenly hid their pupils from them.* (Magazine 21, 1937-38)

In the garden, the boundary wall between Belfield and what had been Elm House was taken down (apart from a curiously shaped piece in the middle of the lawn near to the back of the houses, which contained four lavatory cubicles and some wash basins; this survived until the early 1960s - an archeological puzzle to a generation of LMS girls). What with the devastation that this caused, and the unfinished building, there were grave fears for the 1938 Summer Fete, but Trojan efforts were made, and by July 8th, when the two-day fete was opened by George Lansbury MP, all was ready. The new Kindergarten Room was devoted to an exhibition detailing the history of the two houses that now made up the School. Above this, and the new archway between the houses, were two new classrooms, and on the top floor the new Art Room, all tricked out in an attractive blue and white. A new and separate dining-room had been created in the basement of Lupton House (in what is now the cloakroom beneath the Headmistress's room).

Amidst all the bustle of purchasing, building, and rearranging, it was not overlooked that the School was now celebrating its 21st Birthday. The dedication of the new Chapel, and of the new classrooms and studio, on Saturday, September 24th, 1938, was an appropriate beginning to the occasion. The original 97 pupils had grown to 260, and for the first time in years were comfortably housed. What is more, the LCC had promised to include the long awaited new Hall and Gymnasium in their next Triennium, beginning in 1941.

Lady Margaret School, born amidst so many difficulties and in such dark days, had reached its majority. MB's "particularly happy place" celebrated with all its usual style.

There was the customary Birthday Party, at which the School entertained the Old Girls to a triptych of playlets devoted to the history of the school, in which historical accuracy fell victim to poetic licence (Hamlet and Sir Christopher Wren figured among former pupils of the School, and Mrs Jordan had hysterics because she could no longer find her way round Belfield House since the rebuilding!) The following Thursday, an At Home was held, at which the School proudly showed off its new premises to parents, Old Girls, and friends. The Old Girls held a dinner, at which a proud and thankful MB was Guest of Honour. The week was crowned on Michaelmas Day itself by a Thanksgiving Service at All Saints', Fulham, at which the achievements of the past twenty-one years were remembered with gratitude, humility, and - if truth be told - with something like astonishment that Lady Margaret was still alive and kicking!

The gardens in 1938: looking towards netball courts.

But the school born in the thick of world conflict was soon to know such conflict again. The day of the dedication of the new Chapel was also the day of Munich; Dr Lyttelton, in his 80s and rather frail, was unable to attend the event because of the crisis. Fortunately, however, the "tense atmosphere", as the review of the 21st Birthday celebrations termed it in the Magazine for 1938-39, failed to deter visitors to the At Home. That same week preparations were made to evacuate the entire school out of London, according to the elaborate plans already set in place by the LCC.

The gardens in 1938: looking towards the school.

> *That week, you could have seen most of us struggling to school with cases or rucsacks, rugs or blankets, and mackintoshes or top-coats, not forgetting the gas-masks! Everyone had to bring all necessary kit and food to school. Our rations consisted mainly of tins of corned beef, biscuits, chocolate, and barley sugar. We kept our cases in one room, and scrambled madly over them and each other in our efforts to pack the things we had previously forgotten, or to take away the things that we needed. The stores of food, too, were very useful whenever we felt hungry. We were easily able to obtain a bar of chocolate or anything else from our cases, so long as we renewed the supply overnight. When we were at last able to take our things home again, the room was the scene of a general scrimmage.*
> *(Magazine 22, 1938-39)*

The gardens in 1938: looking towards Elm (Lupton) House.

MB constantly reassured the more timid of the girls, each time an aeroplane flew over. "It is all right, children, no one is going to bomb you."

> *On the Wednesday evening we heard that the crisis had been averted, and we knew that we should not have to evacuate after all. I believe that this was a real disappointment to some of the younger ones who thought it all great fun. Several juniors remarked in sad tones, "Well, aren't we going to evacuate after all?" Most of us, however, were extremely relieved, and I am sure the staff were very thankful that they had not got to be responsible for evacuating about 200 Lady Margaret School girls, together with numbers of their small brothers and sisters.* *(Magazine 22, 1938-39)*

Dancing on the lawn, Summer Fete, 1938.

The gardens in 1938: looking across to the Chirol Wing.

Their relief was temporary, as we all know. That last summer of peace saw the bi-annual School Journey Week. Thirty girls accompanied Miss Winchester to the Lake District for the week, while those remaining at school visited the Housing Exhibition, the Hovis Factory, St Albans, the Tower of London, the British Museum, the London Zoo, and the Regent's Park Open-Air Theatre, to see a performance of *Much Ado About Nothing* - a grimly ironic title in the circumstances. One sign of the times was the presence of four German refugees among the pupils that year. Another was the following:

> *House Committee reported it has dealt with various matters about ARP. The LCC has been asked whether risks to the Caretaker when left in charge would be a public responsibility and not that of the Governors. They had agreed this would be so. The School was not after all needed as an auxiliary Fire Station. There was no part of the building considered safe during an air raid, but since the children would be evacuated, the Committee had not felt any action necessary.* *(Minutes June 23rd, 1939)*

On Sunday, September 3rd, Germany failed to answer the British ultimatum over its invasion of Poland, and war was declared.

Evacuation

For a week before the declaration of war, Lady Margaret, in common with every other London school, had been waiting ready to depart for the comparative safety of the country. The teachers had been recalled from their holidays, and the girls, with a number of little brothers and sisters, waited at school with their luggage packed, just as they had done the year before. The elaborate scheme for the evacuation of children from the capital had been in place for some time, from the moment that the international situation made it likely that there would be war. Adults were to remain, since normal business and production had to be maintained; but the children would be removed as far as possible from danger. Since their teachers would be the one group of adults whose jobs would disappear when the children left, it made sense to organise the removal by schools, so that the teachers could accompany the pupils who represented their employment.

The children would assemble at school with their luggage, and with any non-school-age brothers and sisters who were accompanying them. They would then be taken to the Reception Areas by train, where they would be assigned their billets, that is, put with the families with whom they would be boarding. There was little in the way of finesse about placing children in billets; a certain area would be assessed as having so many available spaces, and that number of children would be assigned. Some children were lucky with what they got, and others were not. It was an ambitious scheme, never before attempted; it operated well enough, but undoubtedly there was much confusion, much petty-fogging bureaucracy, much insensitivity, and much misery. But that is war.

And so Lady Margaret School waited, but not for long. This time it was to be the real thing. Even before that fateful Sunday, the move was under weigh.

> Our evacuation happened on the first Saturday in September, 1939, after a weary week in which we hung about at school with nothing to do, waiting for the word to start. There was a stream of anxious parents to be reassured, small new children to learn, younger and older brothers or sisters to identify. We made lists and checked them, we listened to the wireless. Some sensible people had brought knitting, and knitted incessantly; others wrote letters till they had said all they knew to everyone they could think of; the telephone never stopped, orders and counter orders from County Hall, from local organisers, from traffic superintendents, from Heads of other schools, came in endlessly; but after all only one person at a time can telephone and the others were inevitably and inordinately bored.
> (History, 4th ed. 1967)

The signal came, on that last day of peace, and 201 children, MB and her staff, Miss Lupton, two or three Old Girls, and at least one mother, set off by train from Wimbledon Station. The whole party was set down at Haslemere, and at that point everything started to go wrong. The School had, naturally, asked to be kept together, but the powers-that-be had decided otherwise. The chief concern of the Reception Area officials seemed to be that coaches carrying children from the station did not arrive simultaneously at the same billeting centre. As a result Lady Margaret School was scattered far and wide across Surrey, Sussex and Hampshire to its various billets, and many a girl spent that first night, and the subsequent nights, in a strange bed in a strange house among strange people, without the comfort of her friends and teachers near her. One girl was billeted, with crass insensitivity, with a couple whose two children had not long been killed by enemy action. For many of the girls, too, especially the younger ones, it was their first time ever away from home and family; as they lay there in the dark, they were certainly concerned about parents left behind in London to face whatever horrors Hitler might dispense, and we may be sure that for some it was a tearful introduction to their new homes.

Much of that first term was chaos. The teachers, as is their way in such circumstances, performed miracles of brick-making without the necessary straw. Lessons were started with whatever group of girls could be gathered together: in the public library at Haslemere, in the church hall at Hammer and Hindhead. There were no books to speak of, and improvisation was the order of the day. After the initial shock, one girl at least, thirteen-year-old Jean Prowse, found some positive delight in the regime.

> Actually living in the country, however, was novel to me, and going to school each morning from ten to twelve in the village hall at Hammer, with no homework to do, seemed at the time ideal. The time table consisted mostly of community singing, though I remember Miss Gillard endeavouring to teach French to a number of us ranging from

48

IIIA to VIB [ages 11-17]. It was all very difficult, scattered as we were in various villages.   (Magazine 23, 1945)

One minor flaw in the Government's grand design, so far as it affected Lady Margaret, was that, though they had thoughtfully picked up the whole school from London and found it rooms to sleep in in the country, they had neglected to find it a school in the Reception Area for its pupils to attend! That, apparently, was for the Headmistress and her staff to sort out. MB on her retirement must have had the best girded loins in Christendom, for once more she sprang into action to save her beloved school, fast disintegrating around her.

Miss Moberly Bell was teaching one day when she saw a bus to Midhurst Grammar School. She went there and asked the Headmaster if he would share his school with her pupils. "He asked me if I smoked, and feeling I would be thought of as one of those old schoolma'ams if I refused his cigarette, I accepted, and fortunately wasn't sick. He agreed that I could use his school in the afternoons. He was most cordial, and we shared the school happily for four years.

Midhurst Grammar School, 1992.

"The next thing was to see how many children we could get to the school. I went to see the bus company at Hindhead and asked if I could have a school bus. But they said this was impossible, because of the petrol restrictions. I then asked the Education Department, but they said they couldn't do anything about it. So I went back to the bus company and said, 'Will you let your ordinary passengers know that they will have to be at the bus station an hour before the bus starts, because fifty-three children will be there three-quarters of an hour beforehand?' Soon I received a telephone message from the Sussex Education Department, saying they had arranged for a special bus for the children."   (Magazine 1964-65)

The generous offer by Mr Lucas, Headmaster of the Boys' Grammar School at Midhurst, undoubtedly saved the day. Accommodation for morning lessons were found at Easebourne Priory, a medieval building on the edge of Cowdray Park, an appropriate choice, for it had once been a nunnery. It needed only now for the children's billets to be moved as close as possible to these two sites. The billeting officers, undoubtedly overworked and harrassed, were unwilling to make rearrangements to satisfy some elderly nuisance of a Headmistress from London. Until the following spring, when most of the billets had been changed, the juniors remained in Hindhead for their schooling, while the rest of the school bussed into Midhurst. MB summed up that first term in her report to the Governors at their first war-time meeting.

From September 2nd to November 7th the story was one of continued struggle to undo the harm that had been done at Haslemere station, and get the children rebilleted at Midhurst, where was the nearest Secondary School. 50 children were still miles away from Midhurst, and had to be transported daily by bus.

Midhurst Grammar School had welcomed the school, which was now working half days in its premises, and a building called the Priory at Easebourne had been taken for the children to work in during the mornings.

The whole business of evacuation had been made difficult by division of authority and apparent lack of preparation. Even now it was impossible to get treatment for the eyes and teeth of LCC scholars, because West Sussex declared that no arrangements had been made with them by London
(Minutes, Nov.10th, 1939)

Easebourne Priory, 1992.

That first Christmas of the war, the parents hired motor coaches to bring them all down to Midhurst for a reunion party. There is little doubt that both children and parents found this a cheering, and a saddening, occasion.

When the School had somewhat settled down, it attempted to lead as normal a life as possible. Under the able guidance of Betty Strutt, Head Girl from 1939 to 1941, the

Order continued to function, as did the four divisions, playing each other in a number of sporting fixtures. Joyce Prower won the School's first scholarship to an Art College, a tribute to the excellent teaching of Mrs Lasenby, who later provided the scenery for *Lady Precious Stream*, performed in 1941 by the seniors to an appreciative audience at the Grammar School, and the mural that formed the backdrop for the 1943 production of *Hansel and Gretel*. (Mrs Lasenby was later to paint the portrait of MB which was exhibited at the Royal Academy Summer Exhibition.)

Amidst all the difficulties of evacuation, of living away from home, of constant anxiety about the progress of the war and what might be happening to friends and relatives, of the upsetting of the routine that is a necessary calming influence upon the wayward spirit of youth if it is to learn anything, Lady Margaret School settled down to life at Midhurst. Jean Prowse, looking back over her time at school during this period, had for the most part fond memories of it all.

> *I have innumerable pictures of Midhurst in my mind now, of the striking contrast between the winter and the summer, our mornings at the Priory doing prep., and the long afternoons at the Grammar School; and little things like tobogganing down Whip Hill in winter and picnics on the Downs in summer. The summer was always too short because there was so much we could do. Provided you were not too particular, you could swim in the Rother or go for innumerable rambles or cycles. Chichester was always a popular place for an outing because you could often see quite a recent picture at one of the cinemas and, of course, it possessed an inimitable Woolworths round which you could wander and imagine you were back home.*
>
> *Winter, however, for most of us has the rather morbid picture of an icy Priory, clothes dripping wet, and chilblains, but it has its brighter side in the Grammar School parties and netball matches at Chichester, and even roasting chestnuts in the sixth form fire. If we arrived early at the Priory we used to try to thaw before prayers, because it was so uncomfortable gradually to regain feeling in our hands and feet in church; often in a maths. lesson Miss Winchester would begin with physical jerks, which, incidentally, were enjoyed by everyone....Like everything else we even exaggerated the cold, but we kept ourselves happy just grumbling about it.* (Magazine 23, 1945)

There were of course a great many benefits resulting from the School's new situation. All around them were the wide open spaces of Cowdray Park, in which the Grammar School had its playing fields; Lady Margaret used them for cricket, netball, rounders, and lacrosse. The River Rother ran through the grounds, and a section of it was appropriated for swimming lessons; the water was, of course, unheated, and the muddy banks made getting in and out of the water rather difficult. Some girls borrowed ponies, and spent the day riding across the Downs.

Sharing with the boys' school, which was a boarding school and therefore available throughout the evenings as well, had its advantages. The senior girls were invited to attend the Grammar School Debating Society meetings, and there were lively debates on the pros and cons of evacuation and co-education. Joint musical activities were started with a service of Passion music at Easebourne Church. It perhaps was not merely a love of music that led some of the seniors to form a Beethoven Club!

> *We chose Beethoven as Mr Jackson, music master at the Grammar School, had all nine symphonies on records. We used to gather in his room after school and listen to one each week. Sometimes Mr Jackson talked to us about the composer. I know we all enjoyed these meetings very much, and learned to really appreciate Beethoven.*
> *(War-time Magazine 23, 1939-40)*

The School was fortunate in being placed near the home of the Dolmetch family, the pioneers of the revival of ancient music in this country; at a spring concert at the beginning of 1940 they entertained the School with their home-made recorders, harpsichords, and other Elizabethan instruments.

Then there were the parties. Whatever the attractions of Beethoven in the evenings, clearly Mr Jackson himself had a talent to please, and his contribution to these social gatherings was not despised!

> *The long hours of the blackout were frequently lightened in the winter of the first term, by the boarders of the grammar School.*
> *At the first party everyone was a little shy, but after a few hectic games, such as balloon-busting, the girls and boys had become much more friendly.*
> *It was then decided to form a mixed entertainments committee for the arranging and running of the parties. Three or four girls and boys helped before each party to buy and prepare the food - and many were the headaches incurred whilst trying to feed the guests on fourpence a head.*
> *Separate parties were held for juniors and seniors, and a joint sixth form party was*

held just before Christmas, which was a great success. The decorations were complete in every detail - even to the mistletoe; and the cider-cup made by Mr Jackson was much appreciated.

At the beginning of the second term there were a few parties but these were curtailed owing to the outbreak of various epidemics among the Grammar School boys. This term, however, parties began again with a dance given by our own sixth form for the seniors of both schools. This was voted a very superior affair, particularly as the hall was decorated with rhododendrons, and the guests themselves had become much more proficient in the art of dancing after the lessons given by Mrs Houston.

(War-time Magazine 23, 1939-40)

Friendships sprang up very naturally between members of the two schools. One method (frowned upon!) of initiating a meeting is recalled by Sylvia Thomas (1942-49).

In the classrooms at Midhurst Grammar School we sat in the same desks for basic subjects and registration as our male counterparts. We were strictly forbidden to open the desks because the boys left their property and books in them. However, rumour had it that older girls made assignations with boys by an exchange of notes left in the desks.

There was rather more serious concern about the presence of Canadian airmen and soldiers at a local base. MB and her staff would patrol the streets of Midhurst in the evenings and keep a watchful eye on their precious charges. Diana Gunn (Mrs Glover) (herself the daughter of Vera Sutherland - Mrs Gunn - one of the original Sixth Form of 1917) remembers one such encounter.

On one occasion Miss Bell and Miss Lupton kept the blind date made by a glamorous fifth former and a soldier who to his utter consternation received a dressing-down on his poor choice of a schoolgirl for a man of his age.

Though such incidents are amusing to recall, the constant and unremitting responsibility for their pupils placed upon the staff, in the absence of their parents, was a tremendous burden. As time went by, there was a growing tendency for parents to want to have their children back with them in London, where the dangers were not perceived to be as great as had been at first feared. If the moral dangers to which their daughters were exposed in rural Sussex were thought to be the greater of two evils, there is little doubt that many more would have been brought home, and Lady Margaret School would have died by slow attrition, especially as the LCC was adamant that London schools should remain where they were, whatever individual parents might decide.

The unhappiness suffered by many evacuees is a matter of fact. Though during the day, when they were with their friends, it could all be treated as a big adventure, at home in the billets, with not always the most sympathetic of hosts, it could be utter misery. Some of the host families, who received just eight shillings a week to maintain each child, were none too scrupulous in their use of the children's ration books; there was an outbreak of petty thieving in the summer of 1941, when some younger children, deprived of their sugar ration, were stealing pennies to buy sweets. The absence of Mother was particularly felt by girls entering adolescence:

While we were in our first billet, the girl who was a year older than I was started her periods one night. Neither of us knew what was wrong with her. Our billet lady told her to buy towels from the chemist's on her way home from school. She was too embarrassed to go in so I said I would. I didn't know what she wanted so I bought Meloids, which were tiny black liquorice sweets, which we ate as a change from lemonade powder. She was very irritated with me because she hadn't much money. (Sylvia Thomas)

Living conditions were often primitive in the picturesque country cottages where many of the girls were billeted.

Four of us attempted homework by the light of an oil lamp at the same table where our host skinned and gutted yet another poached rabbit that formed our staple diet. The soil closet in the garden which froze solid as did parts of our anatomy in winter was even less salubrious in summer months with cold water from the pump to do our washing - and no biological powder to help. (Diana Gunn)

My first billet was uncomfortable and unwelcoming. We three children slept in an attic, where the washing water, which we used before school, was literally freezing. Of course there was no bathroom. (Sylvia Thomas)

Though the dangers from enemy action were slight, they were always a possibility, and air raid precautions were a constant feature of life at Midhurst. After Dunkirk, much of the south coast of England became one armed camp, and many of the schools which had been evacuated there were moved elsewhere. Lady Margaret, however, stayed put. Various stratagems were tried for use in the event of an air raid.

At one moment we tried running out to a sunk lane behind the school, but this involved panting across a loose sandypatch, and it took so long to get there that that was tried only once. Then we had a plan of sitting in the boys' cloak rooms crouched under the basins, but the floor was so cold, and we were really very doubtful whether the roof (said to be concrete) gave much shelter. Besides, when the alarm went at 3.30 and the All Clear did not go till 5 or 6 it became from every point of view impossible. Finally we crouched under the desks, or ran home as quickly as we could. (History, 4th ed. 1967)

In February 1943 occurred the most serious incidents. A German plane machine-gunned a local bus full of children, fortunately with no casualties; and on the following day two bombs fell on Midhurst itself. Three Lady Margaret girls were injured, two not seriously, but the Head Girl (who happened to be MB's god-daughter) was cut in the eye by flying glass, and had to be sent to Moorfields for treatment.

By now the pressure to return to London was great. The Governors had, in concert with other similarly placed schools, petitioned the LCC to let them return. Putney High (which of course was not subject to the LCC's diktat) had done so as early as the end of 1939, and there were fears expressed at the Governors' meeting that parents who might have sent their daughters to Lady Margaret would choose that school instead. At a meeting of the Parents' Association on March 3rd, 1940, 32 parents voted to bring their children home immediately, another 32 to do so for September, and only 24 to leave them at Midhurst. The first casualty of the war had been the Kindergarten, which simply ceased to exist; and the rest of the preparatory school could well have followed. Miss Pidwell had indeed gone to Midhurst, but the majority of her class consisted of Midhurst boys rather than Lady Margaret girls. A Kindergarten was opened at Parson's Green, even while the rest of Lady Margaret were still in exile, in an effort to keep the younger part of the school alive; by the summer of 1943, it had 44 children and a waiting list.

That did not solve the problems of the main school. Some parents were removing their daughters at the earliest possible age, fourteen, and sending them to work in London, in order to have them near them, and to take advantage of the high wages available during a labour shortage. Moreover, as the war dragged on, it became all too apparent that the quality of the pupils entering the school at age 11, because of the unsettled nature of their education up to that age, left a lot to be desired. In the end, it was the parents of Lady Margaret who made the decisive move. The Parents' Association met on May 29th, 1943, and all but three decided they would bring their children back to London despite the LCC. The authorities relented, and Lady Margaret, after four years of exile, returned home to its roots.

Return to Parson's Green

Meanwhile, in London the school at Parson's Green still stood, empty and echoing, looked after by the schoolkeeper, Mr Edwards. His wife and little son, Roy, had accompanied the evacuation party in September 1939, and lived in a flat in Easebourne Priory, relatively safe from the threat of bombs.

When the bulk of the School had moved to Midhurst, there remained the problem of the 101 pupils who had not been evacuated. Of these the Headmistress reported at the December 12th, 1939, meeting of the Governors that only 27 were getting satisfactory schooling at other secondary schools. Others were at "inefficient private schools", the rest not in school at all. It was in response to such a situation throughout London, especially when individual children began to drift back to London from the country, that the LCC set up Emergency Schools, to cater for the education of those who chose to brave the bombing. The local one for Fulham was in Fulham County Girls School (what is now Fulham Cross), set up at the beginning of the summer term of 1940. Girls entering Lady Margaret during the war were therefore given a choice: to join the school in Midhurst, or to attend the Emergency School. Sylvia Thomas won a Junior County Scholarship to Lady Margaret in 1942 (value £9 a term for the first year, and £11 a term thereafter), and was interviewed by MB at Parson's Green. She chose Midhurst, as we know. Doreen Hooper (1941-48) chose to attend the Emergency School, and recalls her time there as the unhappiest days of her school life.

One consolation for Lady Margaret girls in Fulham was the presence of two of their own teachers, one of whom was Miss Masaroon. Her arrival at the school shortly before the war had been duly propitious.

> Miss Muir suddenly departed to get married. A Miss Masaroon, age 29, Bristol University I Class Hons: has been appointed temporarily in her place. She is proving so competent that it will probably be well to make her appointment permanent.
> (Minutes, Oct.29th, 1937)

Marjorie Masaroon turned out to be one of that steady stream of outstanding and inspirational teachers that Old Girls remember with affection and gratitude long after they have left school. Under her, English teaching at the school flourished, so that by the time she retired, in 1968, her subject had become the most popular choice in the Sixth Form.

In response to demand from local parents, a small Kindergarten was established at Parson's Green, with about 16 pupils, and work was done to provide air raid protection, at a cost of £21. Even this was under threat, as the numbers were too small.

On October 13th and again on November 29th, the school suffered considerable damage from air raids; windows were blown out, and ceilings brought down. Nothing permanent could be done by way of repairs, but first aid in the shape of boarding up was carried out. Another source of damage was the local Fulham Home Guard, who used the premises as their headquarters from the beginning of 1941. Apart from the usual wear and tear of not over-scrupulous soldiery with their boots and equipment, the oak-panelling in the school was soon riddled with dart holes, Mr Edwards had school linen taken from his flat, and, to crown it all, there was soon a regular trade in stolen science equipment from the laboratory, in particular some rather expensive microscopes. MB was actually summoned as a witness to the court-martial of one of the offenders, but the case could not be proved and nothing was ever recovered.

All this added fuel to the Governors' campaign to have the School return to Parson's Green. By 1942 the numbers at Midhurst were just over 130, with perhaps another 40 in emergency schools in London. Work was progressing well, in the circumstances, girls entering and passing their General and Higher Schools in surprisingly healthy numbers. Doing examinations required some juggling; the Higher candidates for 1941 went to Bedales for their examination. In 1942, Rosemary Gee delighted everyone in the midst of the gloom by winning an Exhibition at Girton. By 1943 the numbers had dropped again, and at last the LCC began to soften its hard line.

> The Head Mistress had asked for an interview with Dr Hughes at County Hall, and in discussion with him had been given leave to open the Preparatory Department in London after Easter, provided 30 children were enrolled. The Home Guard had been

asked to vacate the necessary rooms, and the architect instructed to put them in order. There seems little doubt that the requisite number of children will be produced. Miss Thorpe, who has been on loan to another school, will take charge.

Prospects for September: The LCC also said that classes could be opened at Parson's Green for any children back in London, but no parent must be advised to bring her child home. If a sufficient number remained in Midhurst, educational facilities must be provided for them there. The Head Mistress was meeting the Parents' Association to discuss the position in a week's time. (Minutes, Feb.12th, 1943)

The newly opened Preparatory school soon had 44 children, and a waiting-list, and, to help teach them, Miss Pidwell had to be summoned home from Midhurst, where she had a class consisting of twenty Midhurst children and only ten Lady Margaret ones. The parents' decision on May 29th settled the affair, and Lady Margaret gathered itself together once more in September on its own beloved premises.

It was a sad picture of dilapidation and neglect. The railings along the road front were gone, replaced with straggling barbed wire, windows were boarded up, paint was peeling, dirt and dust were everywhere. The Staff, returned from their various wartime locations, were tired with the exertions of evacuation, when even their evenings and holidays had to be devoted to the supervision of the pupils. MB herself fell ill the moment that she could afford to, and Mrs Dalton acted in her place for much of the Autumn term in 1943. Miss Phillips, another of the original staff, was still going, but clearly not strong; at the end of the first term back in London she had a serious breakdown and was ordered a temporary rest, from which she never in fact returned. Miss Carver, a member of the Governing Body from the very beginning, had moved out of London during the war, and now felt it time to retire. Miss Lupton, who, though not even a paid member of staff, had stalwartly coped alongside the professionals at Midhurst, felt it necessary to lay down the burdens of Clerk to the Governors, which she had held since taking over from Mrs Bell in 1926. Her parting gift was to present the Governors with the freehold of Elm House.

At least two of the staff elected to remain in Sussex. Miss Nicholson, who had been much involved in the dramatic productions at Midhurst, had found a teaching job in Chichester. Mrs Lasenby, her helpmate in those productions, had two daughters of her own whom she did not want to bring back to London, and her husband had work in Sussex. Miss Winchester took the opportunity of the move back to London to accept a post at Chertsey; MB echoed the *cri de coeur* that later Headmistresses were to be familiar with, that replacement "Mathematics teachers were practically unobtainable", but by good fortune she found Miss Mobbs to take her place.

The School re-opened at Parson's Green with 104 children, about 65 of whom had been at Midhurst. By January 1944, there were 223, but with the beginning of the V-1 rocket raids - the notorious "doodle-bugs" - in February, numbers fell off sharply to around eighty. That summer, the July public examinations were "done to the accompaniment of flying bombs", as the Headmistress phrased it in her report; examinations were done in the Geography Room (now the Head's room), with Mr Edwards on guard in the garden outside waving to the invigilator when he thought the girls should take cover under their desks. Despite all this, ten of the sixteen General Schools candidates were successful, and four of the six Highers. Four pupils went on to Training Colleges, one to University, and another to the Royal College of Music with a Scholarship. Term ended a week early, because of the bombing, and many of the seniors spent the vacation at an agricultural camp in Lincolnshire organised by Mrs Dalton. Things were better by September 5th, when the new term began with 107 children, rising to nearly two hundred by the end of the month. (September 5th was a very early start, and two days extra half-term were given by the Governors to prevent its being a very long term!) By half-term February 1945, numbers had risen to 230, by April 250, and by September (by which time the war had ended), the 300 mark had been passed, the largest number in the School's history to that date.

So the war ended. Battered and weary, Lady Margaret could pause to lick its wounds and survey the scene. The previous six years had not passed without loss. Mrs Sharp, from Whitelands days, mother of Gladys and Muriel, and a constant support in the early days at Parson's Green, had been killed by a bomb in Westminster in March 1941. Joan Ironside, Head Girl in 1929-30 (sister of Margaret, Head Girl 1924-25), died in 1943, when her home in Putney was hit. Another victim of the war was Winifred Barnes (last Head Girl at Whitelands 1916-17), who, never a strong person physically, gave so much of herself as a LCC Care Committee worker, organising the evacuation of London school-children, that she suffered a breakdown in 1940; from this she never fully recovered, the end of the war saw her an invalid still, and she died early in 1953, aged 53.

(Winifred had, in fact, transferred to Parson's Green for a year, to receive coaching for University; she was No.1 in the School Register.)

The war had seen Lady Margaret girls in service for their country. Those at school in Sussex regularly spent summer holidays in harvesting, and weekends in the autumn lifting potatoes for the local farmers. Many Old Girls, and those leaving school during the war, joined the forces - the ATS (as the women's branch of the army then was) and the WAAFs (later the Women's Royal Air Force) - or performed other necessary tasks like driving ambulances or doing ARP work. Athena Adamson was a nurse in Basra, and Dora Jelley in Colombo; Phyllis Ruegg was an officer in the ATS, Joan Whitlock helped "man" the anti-aircraft guns around the coast, and Pixie Ward (who had performed for the Princess back in 1918) hung up her dancing shoes and joined the WAAF.

But even as the war dragged to a close, the shape of the subsequent peace was already being marked out. A White Paper on "Educational Reconstruction" was put out by the Government in 1943, which declared in ringing tones, "Upon the education of the people of this country the fate of this country depends." This was to lead to the Education Act of 1944, carried through by Mr R A Butler, President of the Board of Education in the war-time Coalition Government (two of whose grand-daughters were to be pupils in the School in the 1970s). Its provisions were designed to have the profoundest effect upon the schools of this country - including Lady Margaret School - for another generation.

"A sad picture of dilapidation and neglect" - the School in 1943.

Brave New World

The 1943 White Paper, and the 1944 Act which resulted from it, were very much the product of the titanic conflict through which the country was then passing. A determination to build a new and better world for the coming generations manifested itself in a vision of an educational system that took each child for at least ten years and realised all the talents that were in him.

> *The war has revealed afresh the resources and character of the British people - an enduring possession that will survive all the material losses inevitable in the present struggle. In the youth of the nation we have our greatest national asset. Even on the basis of mere expediency, we cannot afford not to develop this asset to the greatest advantage. It is the object of the present proposals to strengthen and inspire the younger generation. For it is as true today, as when it was first said, that "the bulwarks of a city are its men".*
>
> *(White Paper on Educational Reconstruction. 1943)*

The Act that followed implemented this aim by insisting that every child - and not just the few who could afford the fees or win a Junior County Scholarship - should receive Secondary Education (which was now defined as the second stage of education, from the age of 11, after the first stage, the primary schools, which were to cater for the 5-11s). Provision was made to raise the school-leaving age from 14 to 15 (this was done in 1947), and eventually to 16, so that every child would receive at least four years of secondary schooling.

The problem was that the pre-war secondary school (such as Lady Margaret) was essentially an academic institution, whose function was to prepare its pupils for public examinations (the School Certificate) and, for the very best, entrance to university and training colleges. Perhaps a fifth or a quarter of eleven-year-olds were intellectually able to take that road. If the rest of the child population was to receive "secondary education", it was not going to be Latin and trigonometry. Hence the phrases in the White Paper - "not of a single pattern", "diversity", "diversified types but of equal standing", "parity of esteem". There would be other sorts of secondary school besides the existing ones, which were now dubbed Secondary Grammar Schools. Those providing a general education to the majority of the population, without the School Certificate at the end of it, were christened Secondary Modern Schools; unfortunately, they were often no more than the old senior elementary schools, housed in the same buildings, with the same pupils and staff that they had had previously. Between these two was to be found in some parts of the country the Secondary Technical School, founded to repair the perceived failure to develop the technical skills of the nation as compared with the Germans, a lesson rammed home by the war. Where they could be found (the Stanley School in Croydon, for instance), they enjoyed considerable prestige, something which the secondary modern quite failed to do. Children were no longer to be selected (or not) for secondary education; instead, a series of aptitude tests (the "11-plus") would determine what kind of secondary schooling was best suited to the talents of each individual child. The working-class child would no longer lose out because of his poverty or his poor showing at an interview; he stood as good a chance of a grammar school place as anyone, and if he did not, one secondary school was as good as another.

Or so the theory ran. It is true that more working-class children got to grammar schools than had previously been the case, but they remained for the most part thoroughly middle-class institutions, with a disproportionate percentage of their pupils coming from the skilled artisan and managerial classes; and, conversely, the new "modern" schools seemed to attract few of such pupils. The socialist tide was running; the sweeping Labour victory in the General Election of 1945 opened the way to greater radicalism in the interpretation of the 1944 Act, and the great metropolitan areas, with radical Labour authorities, were determined to push ahead. What if, they asked, instead of providing different secondary schools to complement and supplement the old type, we expanded the old type to include the whole range of ability of secondary school age? Thus was born the concept of the comprehensive school.

It is against this background that Lady Margaret was to live the next thirty years of its life. Increasingly, there grew up a strong feeling in the country that an academically selective school was divisive, elitist, an affront in an equal society. Those who felt this way looked to the comprehensive school to cure all that was rotten in British society - its class-ridden structures and its social fragmentation. In the comprehensive school, dustman's child would rub shoulders with duke's child, each would learn to respect the other, and none would be labelled second-rate because he had failed to enter the right institution at eleven.

One particular effect of the 1944 Act was to redefine the relationship of the Aided Schools (mostly Church Schools such as Lady Margaret) with the local educational authorities. Hitherto such schools had done rather well, having many of their costs met by public funds, yet retaining a great deal of independence. Henceforth, such schools would have to decide between becoming Voluntary Controlled Schools, which continued to be fully funded from the public purse, or to elect for Voluntary Aided status, which would preserve their old freedoms, but make them liable for much more of their own costs.

With the approach of the end of the war, MB looked forward to fulfilling her building plans with the completion of the new Hall and Gymnasium; the LCC, it will be remembered, had agreed to include these in their next building project. The war put a stop to that, and when it was all over the scene had changed entirely. MB wrote ruefully:

> In 1938, when we took possession of Elm House, and got our plans for completing our buildings; when the LCC said they would, in the next triennium, give us the money we needed for the new Hall, gymnasium and class-rooms, I thought our financial troubles were over. I thought that by 1943 or 44, the buildings would be really complete, that we should have a grand opening ceremony, after which I should retire, handing over a lovely school to a younger and more competent successor.
>
> Well, it hasn't happened like that. The "next triennium" was fully occupied with the war and the new Education Act has made it impossible for the LCC to give us any money for building unless we become a "controlled" school. The governors have decided - and I am sure you will be glad about this - to keep the independence of the school. But of course we must pay to have the buildings, and since the LCC cannot pay, we must. The Ministry of Education will pay half the cost, and our half will amount to about £10,000.
>
> (Magazine 23, 1945)

And so the Building Fund was re-launched - had it indeed ever put into harbour? By the end of a year the first thousand had been collected; collecting the next nine should prove "a trivial affair", wrote MB.

The immediate post-war cocerns of the school - the provisions of the 1944 Act, Aided status, the need to expand, the need for new buildings and more room - were inextricably entwined. The LCC wanted the school to be two forms of entry at age 11, and to do this the preparatory department would need to close; the Governors reluctantly agreed, the junior school was allowed to grow itself out, and Miss Pidwell, who had served it faithfully throughout the School's existence, took the opportunity to retire, in 1947. (The very last girl to have been in the prep. was Caitlin Hughes; she left in July 1959, and subsequently took vows as a member of the Community of the Holy Name at Malvern.) The money with which to build the facilities required was dependent on the status the school chose for itself; but the Association of Governors of Aided Schools (to which Lady Margaret belonged) were anxious not to act hastily in this, and no immediate decision could be made. (Indeed, it was not finally concluded until April 1951, and until then the School existed in a kind of legalistic limbo, unofficially connected to the Diocese of London through the fact that the Bishop of Kensington was Chairman of Governors.) Moreover, building new facilities was increasingly dependent upon acquiring new space, and just as in the 1930s eyes had been cast next door upon Elm House, so now they were being cast next door again, upon Henniker House. (This was the property of the LCC, having been a children's home. What is now the Music Room was a large communal bathroom, with half-a-dozen baths and lavatories.) The School's status as a grammar school was also in question; the LCC's immediate reaction to the 1944 Act was to suggest to the Governors that they might like to assist in the forming of a "multilateral" (i.e. comprehensive) school on the Parson's Green site (Minutes, Oct. 10th, 1944).

The abolition of fee-paying by the 1944 Act led to the LCC's having much more say in the school's recruitment. Now of the 50 new entrants for 1945, 40 were to be children sent by the Authority, and only ten were to be "Governors' places". There was a further move by the LCC to incorporate Lady Margaret into its grand scheme. The Governors had rejected the LCC's proposal that Lady Margaret should become a comprehensive school, arguing the need for every area of the capital to have one or two "exceptional" schools, where children who might not fit into the pattern of the Grand Design could attend; they undoubtedly had academic bias in mind when they used the term "exceptional", but also the need for small, family-sized units, rather than the large institutions being envisaged. Now another idea was mooted; grammar schools would have built alongside them schools taking the rest of the academic range, and the two schools between them would act as a comprehensive unit. These schools would be known as "County Complementary Schools"; Lady Margaret was to be partnered by Hurlingham School, then in Hugon Road, until its successor was built. There was some unease among the Governors over this proposal; they were anxious not to compromise their independence, and they sought clarification of the precise legal relationshiop between the two two schools.

> *The London County Council were represented by Dr Brooks and Miss Blackwell. Dr Brooks informed the Governors that the Council proposed that the Lady Margaret School should continue to provide grammar school education in the South Fulham area; that it should retain its own identity and Head Mistress; that it should be associated with a new school to be built in the Hurlingham district for about 900 to 1000 pupils and that Lady Margaret and this new school should be considered one "comprehensive unit".*
>
> *Until such time as the new school should be built it was suggested that this "federation" with the Hurlingham School should at once be begun.*
>
> *The Head Mistress asked what was meant by "federation"? Dr Brooks replied that "cooperation" might be a better word; that it was hoped that amenities should be shared and cooperation established between the staffs. The Head Mistress pointed out that she had space neither in school nor playing field to share with anyone, nor was it possible to share staff. Dr Brooks replied that all that was necessary was friendliness, and stated that the sooner this could be begun the better. The Head Mistress said this presented no difficulties.* (Minutes, Oct.23rd, 1945)

The friendliness and cooperation with Hurlingham bore immediate fruit; a joint Junior Choir was instituted, which won a first class certificate, along with Lady Margaret's other two choirs, in the London Schools' Music Festival the following year.

MB's somewhat astringent references to "space" at that meeting were clearly made for a purpose, for she enlisted Dr Brooks's aid there and then in the School's pursuit of Henniker House! By September 1946 there were 345 children in the school, and over-crowding was acute. Morning assembly was held in shifts, a senior and a junior following one after the other. The little dining-room held fifty children; yet well over two hundred required school lunches. The Council offered to put up a prefabricated kitchen and dining-hall at the end of the garden; as this would cover one of the two net-ball courts it was not accepted. Eventually, the juniors only were fed on the premises, while the older girls were sent to Ackmar Road and King's Road Schools for their lunch. The Vicar of St Dionis' offered his church hall for lessons, but it was considered quite unsuitable. The LCC put forward plans to rebuild the site completely, but the Governors refused point-blank to have the historic houses destroyed, a stand for which generations of Lady Margaret girls must be extremely grateful!

"Hansel and Gretel" 1948. Sylvia Thomas as the Witch, Katherine Polge on Gretel's left.

End of an era

And while all this was going on, the school got on as best it could with the daily round and common task. The first priority was the welding of the confused mass of Midhurst returners, ex-Emergency Schoolers, and totally new entrants into a school again, with Lady Margaret ways of thinking and behaving. Doreen Hooper, after two years at the Emergency School, found it something of a culture shock; she joined LMS on its return from Midhurst, "fully prepared to be as naughty as I was previously", but she was soon disabused.

Not that Lady Margaret girls were always little angels.

> Just after we arrived back from Midhurst we founded a secretish society called the Keyhole Kates, named after a character in a favourite comic. At the end of the playground was the gardener's hut with a broken lock on the door. We met in there regularly to investigate injustice and crime. We wore badges in the shape of a keyhole. I'm not sure we achieved many of our stated aims but friendships between the Midhurst girls and the Fulham girls were made and have lasted till this day.   (Sylvia Thomas)

Doreen Hooper, although she was a member of the Order and should have known better, got fed up with fire drills!

> On this last occasion several of us hid in the cupboards - some lying on shelves - in order not to be found. Miss Gillard came and tapped very gently on the door of the Order Room. I am sure she knew we were there - it was very difficult not to giggle. I think she may have looked in but she went away again. I do not know how many of us were packed like sardines or how our absence was explained.

One particular excitement attached to fire drills was the tubular chute by which girls descended from the first-floor laboratory onto the street below. This had been installed in the early 1920s, but still gave pleasure to succeeding generations of Lady Margaret girls. Doreen Hooper again:

> On my first introduction to this contraption my form was engaged in netball in the playground, so we had to descend dressed in navy blue knickers (with a pocket for one's handkerchief) irrespective of the fact that we ended up in the road. Also on this occasion one of the girls who was rather large (not her fault - glandular, I believe) got stuck. I think after a lot of pulling, pushing and shaking she emerged once more. It must have been a very nasty experience for her though.

With the return to Parson's Green, the four divisions, which had been suspended in 1942 in Midhurst, were revived, and hotly disputed sporting fixtures resumed their place on the scene. The Staff v. School netball match in 1946 resulted in the injury of Miss Scrivenor, who was off school for some time thereafter! Outings and visits began again with all their pre-war vigour. To mark the end of the war, the LCC had laid on "treats" for the schools of London; on the appointed day, June 14th, 1946, Lady Margaret seniors attended the ballet at Sadlers Wells, while the juniors went to the circus at Wembley. MB did not stop there; a cousin of hers was the manager of the Royal Albert Hall, and she had wangled tickets for most of the School to attend the "Drums" Pageant there.

Drama had not come to a halt because of the war; the production of *Hansel and Gretel* at Midhurst had drawn an audience not only from the two schools, but also from the town itself. In the summer of 1946, the Sixth Form presented *Alcestis*. Senior and middle-school drama groups were formed, and plays put into production, including a revival of *Hansel and Gretel* for the benefit of the many who had not been at Midhurst. The Nativity Tableaux, so much a feature of pre-war School life, were revived, and the School's various religious and charitable organisations continued to flourish; the Mission at Ekutuleni, serving Orlando and Sophiatown in South Africa, founded by Bishop Maud's daughter, had been the School's especial charity since the Bishop's death in 1932, and continued to receive its support. School journeys were resumed - a camp at Hindhead, and another the following year at Ockenden, for the Lower IVs (12-13 year olds), trips to Belgium and Paris - and all appeared to be back to normal.

MB, now in her thirtieth year as Headmistress of the School she had founded, had hoped to retire in 1943 or 1944, with all the building and expansion finished, and a successful, thriving, and spacious school to hand on to her chosen successor. The war had put paid to that dream, as it did to many others. Now, much was still to do, the new Hall, gym, and classrooms were still several thousands of pounds away, and time was not standing still. The Governors were informed, at their meeting in June 1946, that in the following March Miss Moberly Bell would be 65, and due to retire. The School was still picking itself up from the effects of the war, and neither MB nor the Governors were happy about a change of Head just yet. The authorities said Christmas 1946, and the School said no. But the inevitable had to be, sooner or later, and on February 18th 1947, four candidates for MB's post were interviewed, and 36-year-old Miss Florence Elsie Marshall, a mathematics graduate of Durham University, who had been teaching at Lincoln High School under the eminent Miss Savill, was appointed to succeed her the following September.

Lady Margaret owed much to Enid Moberly Bell; above all, it owed her its very existence. Through thirty ceaseless years, the boundless faith and energy of this woman had brooked no opposition, had entertained no doubts, had held fast to the conviction that the God who was the very source of her being would preserve this well-loved child of hers because it deserved to live. She had seen it struggle like a new-born chick from its fragmented shell at Chelsea, and had led it safe through all difficulties, opposition, and tribulations - finding a home, raising money, gathering friends, seeking out room for growth, shepherding her flock through the chaos and conflagration of the war - only to find it jeopardised by schemes and upheavals of a very different kind, but which could affect its existence just as decisively as any V-2 rocket.

The tributes flowed fast and thick throughout 1947. Gladys Sharp had been a 12-year-old at Whitelands when MB arrived to be her Form Mistress; and when the School moved to Parson's Green she came with it as a teacher.

> *From the age of 12 or 13, when she came to be my form-mistress, I have never ceased to have the greatest respect and affection for M.B.; her courage and understanding, sympathy, humour, and charm, and above all her integrity.*
>
> *It was a comparatively new idea in those days that, even if one were not intellectual or brilliant, one could be of use in the world in many other ways. MB, while keeping a wary eye on the ninety and nine, took infinite trouble over the one that appeared to be lost - the awkward, the shy, the apparently unlovable. How many of us have blessed her for this quality.* (Magazine 25, 1946-47)

Jeannie Griffiths (1925-33) recalls her stimulating presence and personality.

> *MB and Miss Lupton in the summer holidays rented a farmhouse in Cornwall for a month, and on leaving school I was fortunate in being invited two or three times to spend two blissful weeks in their company. The party consisted of about ten or so and included were her nephews and cousins and my brothers. After having conventional family holidays in polite seaside resorts on safe beaches, it was an adventure to explore Cornish cliffs and the moors and to go for long walks with them. We talked endlessly on all subjects under the sun, had lovely picnics and bathing from rocky beaches, and the evenings were filled with solving "The Times" crosswords and family games. In those days it was a constant delight just to be in her company, to be stimulated by her conversation and her unexpected outlook on life, not always accepting the conventional social mores as being right and proper.* (Magazine 1967)

This "unexpected outlook" had caused some heart-burning in Phyllis Gardner (1928-35), when she was 15, and therefore with strong feelings on most matters.

> *I remember when the Bishop of Kensington, "Bishop Maud", was dying, MB prayed at Prayers for "an easy passing". I was so furious at what seemed to me to be her lack of faith in not praying for his recovery even at that stage. I went in during break and told her how extraordinarily lacking in faith this seemed. As always, she let one have one's complete outpouring even if it was against her! It was only later that I realized how very much Bishop Maud meant to her, and how this must have hurt her; and even later did I realize what an unusual thing this was to be able to do to the Headmistress.*
> (Magazine 1967)

MB handed over her precious bundle, one suspects, with regret and reluctance. Her last act was to prepare for her successor a sheaf of detailed notes on "how she had done things", in the hope, no doubt, that "things" would continue as they always had done. Changes, however, come willy-nilly, as they had even in her own day, and reading those notes, a Lady Margaret girl of today would hardly recognise the school they describe so minutely. But the capacity to change is a guarantee of continuing life, as MB herself so clearly saw in the final paragraph of her School History.

> *There is another thing about a heritage. You receive it, and you hand it on. Today the School is entrusted to us, it is a living, growing thing, it will become what we make it. When the day comes for us to hand it on, may we have deserved the blessing pronounced on the "good and faithful servants" who have increased the talent entrusted to them.*

New Broom

The new Headmistress was born in the year that MB began teaching at Whitelands College School, and was six years old when Lady Margaret School was founded. She was in fact the same age at the start of her Headship as MB had been. Elsie Marshall came from a northern family which was as obscure as MB's had been constantly in the limelight. Her father had been a railwayman, her mother a great cook; her death in 1919 from influenza, when Elsie was still a small girl, and his from a lingering cancer when she was a young woman, proved to be the fires that merely hardened the steel of her Christian conviction. In many ways her experience of life was closer to that of many of the pupils of Lady Margaret than MB's had been; Miss Marshall had made her own way, with no connections, no family capital, needing to work from economic necessity.

She had had a happy school life, and it was at school that she developed a great love of reading, inspired by "one of those wonderful English teachers who have the gift of opening windows in the minds of their pupils" (Magazine 1971). Her background among some of the poorest in the country gave her a concern for social matters and an intense desire to provide opportunities for advancement for the very humblest, if they had the ability; it was therefore not a contradiction in her that she supported strongly throughout her Headship the retention of the School's academic selectivity.

She began teaching at West Leeds High School, intending to gain some experience before embarking on a career in training colleges. School teaching, however, she found more attractive, and in 1938 was persuaded by Miss Savill of Lincoln High School to take a post with her. She had just resigned her position there, intending to realise a long-held desire to embark upon a degree in Theology, when her appointment to the Headship of Lady Margaret interrupted this plan, and in fact, she afterwards would ruefully say, she never did have a moment to resume it.

Lady Margaret, she recalled, was hardly a welcoming proposition.

> At first sight, battered after the war years and bleak with cold in that severe winter, the school was scarcely attractive and yet it at once clutched my heart strings and has held them ever since.
> (Magazine 1971)

The most pressing need was for more space and more building. As Miss Marshall began her first term, the Rebuilding Fund stood at just short of £2000; this amount was the limit allowed by the National Savings Scheme in one of their accounts and alternative investments had to be found, for other offers were even then being made, including one of £500 by an Old Girl if the School could raise a similar amount. This objective was pursued with gusto; the planned production of Humperdinck's opera, *Hansel and Gretel*, eventually realised in the summer of 1948, raised a useful £22 towards it. Sylvia Thomas gave a spirited performance as the Witch; another part was played by her friend Katherine Polge, who shortly after leaving school married the writer and poet Laurie Lee, author of *Cider with Rosie* (see p.58).

Sylvia Thomas was responsible for another scheme to raise money for the rebuilding.

> During my last two years we had a flourishing Twelve Voice Choir. We had managed to collect twelve of the old barathea red and black striped blazers which hadn't been made since the war started, and these were lent to members to wear. One Christmas we asked if we could go out carol-singing in aid of the Rebuilding Fund ... We went to the Earl's Court area and sang through our repertoire many times, and collected a lot of money. Towards the end of the evening a youngish man came down some steps of a typical large terraced house and asked us if we would go to the top and sing to his sick wife. Then he told us she loved our singing and that this would probably be her last Christmas. We climbed the stairs and sang all our songs, but some of us were very choked up. He insisted on making a contribution, and when we came down again we went home with hardly a word.

(Sylvia Thomas later married and became Mrs Truckle, and her son Martin came as a temporary teacher to the school for a year in 1990.)

The LCC came up with various schemes in order to accommodate the School on its cramped site. The Kitchen and Dining Hut idea, which the Governors had already rejected, was floated again; as was an ambitious scheme to bulldoze a dozen houses in Delvino Road which backed onto the school, in order to build along there. This was felt not to be be very practical.

Sylvia Thomas (on left) and Sheila Feathers in their pre-war blazers 1947.

Then came the news that the LCC were planning to close down the Home in Henniker House and move the children elsewhere. Canon Tirrell, the Diocesan Board representative on the Governing Body, agreed to pursue the possibility, long dreamed of by Lady Margaret School, that the vacated premises might be acquired for the expansion programme. That was in February 1950. By July hope seemed to be fading, and at the end of the year there was vague talk of turning it into a training school for nurses. A welcome gift of £500 from the National Society towards refurbishing any new premises seemed a joke in rather poor taste! But things were still moving under the surface, and eventually the breakthrough came; at the Governors' Meeting of May 28th, 1951, it was announced that the LCC had agreed to hand over the coveted prize. And on this occasion there was no need for a Miss Lupton and her copper mine shares; the Diocesan Board expressed themselves willing to buy the property, and to present it to the School as a gift. Canon Tirrell, who perhaps had been at his most persuasive in the case, announced that a 50% grant would be forthcoming from the Ministry of Education for any necessary rebuilding and alteration.

Meanwhile, the London Development Plan rumbled on, with its long-term aim of making the entire public education service of the capital comprehensive in character. Faced with the Governors' blank refusal to cooperate in changing the nature of the School, the LCC pursued its "county complementary" idea. There was some dissension even over this in the early 1950s, when the new school (now Hurlingham and Chelsea, in Peterborough Road) was being built, since the Council persisted in referring to it as the "Lady Margaret Complementary School" - in all good faith, no doubt, for that that was its intended purpose - but the Governors were uneasy about the use of the School's name for an institution over which they had no control. The Governors suggested it might be called "Moberly School", thus associating it with Lady Margaret, while at the same time pointing out the difference. (A similar line of thought gave the name "Dick Sheppard", after a famous Vicar of St Martin-in-the-Fields, to the complementary school for St Martin's at Tulse Hill.) This was turned down; it seemed that the LCC already had a Moberly School. "Lyttelton School" was offered instead. But in the end, when the new school was built, it kept its old name, Hurlingham.

The other fall-out from the 1944 Act was the School's status as an Aided School. In common with all other schools in a similar position, it had been sent the notorious Form 18, which it found impossible to complete and return without fully exploring its implications. The business dragged on for some years, the School existing in an ambiguous position the meantime, but at last all was settled, and the Governors, at their meeting on March 10th, 1951, were informed that Aided status had been granted, with effect from April 1st. This did not stop the LCC attempting to acquire a veto on Staff appointments (Minutes, Oct.12th, 1951), but the Governors politely saw them off.

Miss Marshall's main concern, coming as she did from the highly academic Lincoln High School, was to raise the academic standing of her new charge. There were several things to be done in this respect. First, the unacceptable practice of girls leaving at 15 had to be stopped; the School had no legal powers to prevent parents removing their children at this age, but what could be done by persuasion and pressure was done. Parents were reminded of the contract they had made with the School and the LCC when their daughters had gained a place at a grammar school, to keep them in school at least until they had finished the course as far as General Schools (or, after 1951, GCE "O" level); and an imposing member of the Governing Body would be set to interview the offending parents, with a view to shaming them into keeping their bond. It has to be said that these methods did not work, and it was only with a general change of attitude and social climate that the practice ceased. Another incentive was the introduction of the School Diploma, for those Fifth Formers who would not be taking the new GCE "O" level; when this examination was first introduced, it was set at a higher standard than the old General Schools, and considered to be above the capabilities even of many pupils attending grammar schools.

The next target was the Sixth Form. Only a minority of girls continued their education into the Sixth Form; in September 1948, it had 25 members altogether. Of these, only one was studying for Higher Schools (what was to become GCE "A" level), while the rest pursued newly introduced Commercial and Nursing courses. Miss Marshall grasped the nettle, and insisted on a written contract from parents, before accepting their child, that she would stay the full six- or seven-year course, and not merely until she was 16. At the same time the academic syllabus was strengthened and broadened. A General Inspection by the Ministry of Education in April 1948 praised MB's hard work during the war in keeping the School going as well as she did, but Mr Hickie, the chief inspector, had some hard words to say about the Staff; they were all very conscientious, but, with two exceptions, were "not outstandingly good teachers". That was something that Miss Marshall, as the opportunities presented themselves, strove to put right in her appointments to the Staff. By 1953 the numbers in the Sixth Form had risen to over 40, and in that year an increased number had gained places at universities, one had got into Oxford, and a State Scholarship had been awarded. Miss Boundy was doing great things in the Art Department, and the number of girls going on to Art Colleges grew. Linda Console, appointed to the Modern Languages department in 1948, took French under her wing and propelled it forcefully into success. Her methods were not always appreciated by her pupils, for she could be quite ruthless with those who failed to measure up to her demanding standards; but girls began degree courses in French in increasing numbers, and it became a matter of some surprise when at least two girls in the school did not win the coveted, fiercely contested LCC Modern Language Travel Scholarships each year. The completion of a new advanced laboratory meant that, from September 1953, Physics could be introduced to the School's syllabus. At the same time, the non-"A" level courses were "beefed up"; the nursing course was given added rigour (and greater commercial value) by taking girls up to Part 1 standard of the Preliminary State Nursing examination. By the 1960s, the policy had worked so effectively that there were well over a hundred in the Sixth Form, more than a quarter of the School's pupils.

When the School eventually acquired Henniker House in 1951, it wasted no time in laying claim to the new premises. School lunches were immediately transferred to its dining room, as if by eating there an inalienable proprietorship should be established. With the house, of course, came the garden, running the full length of the School's existing grounds. Here, it was hoped, would be built the long-awaited new Hall, where once more the entire School could gather in one space for its morning worship and other assemblies. The LCC were asked to include this project in their next building plans; but this, for various legalistic reasons, was not for the present possible. In the meantime, there was Henniker House to be enjoyed.

Henniker House, so named by the LCC just before the war in memory of Mrs Joan Henniker, a local MP, had until then simply been No.9, Parson's Green. Like Elm and Belfield Houses, it occupied the site of earlier houses dating back to the 14th century. It was called "Stowte's tenement", after its original owner, and its first recorded mention is in the minutes of a Court General for 1391. In the following century, it was in the possession of Gerald Hokelem, who died in 1422, and then his daughter Agnes, wife of William Conyngton. The Parker family held it for the first half of the 16th century, and the Dodds thereafter.

There followed a succession of owners, several of them Rectors of Chelsea. The old house was pulled down at the end of the 17th century, and a new house, Albion House, or "The White House", was built. From 1714 to 1725 it was the residence of a Lady Temple. In 1797, it was acquired by Mr William Maxwell, who opened it as a boarding school for boys. Albion House School closed about 1828, when the property was purchased by Mr John Daniel, pulled down, and replaced by the present building, then known as Park House. This mansion was erected by Messrs Cubitt about 1841. Squire Daniel is reputed to have designed it so that it might last a thousand years. Some of the floors were built of solid oak.

At the end of the 19th century it was acquired by the Fulham Poor Law Guardians for boarding pauper children. It continued under various changes in the structures of local government to fulfil this function, until eventually the LCC agreed to let Lady Margaret have it.

Miss Moberly Bell was approached for her permission to have the new house named after her, as a solid memorial to her thirty years' work; this she gave, and the School set to the task of refurbishment.

> There are few pleasures greater than that of planning a new building to meet your desires and fulfil your dreams. Staff and girls revelled in it. Miss Boundy planned all the colour schemes and they were new and exciting; the Staff spread itself in two comfortable rooms [what are now Rooms 4 and 5], leaving their old cramped premises to make craft rooms for the art department. Moberly Bell House has also provided us with four new class rooms and a beautiful Domestic Science Room [Room 34], as well as ample kitchen and dining space so that meals can be cooked on the spot, instead of being brought in all tasting of the containers. (History, 4th ed. 1967)

Joy Boundy had been appointed in April 1950, and she remained until her retirement in 1976. In that time she did for Art in the school what Miss Masaroon did for English; her boundless joy in her subject proved infectious, and Art became, and so remains, one of the glories of the school. She was alive with ideas - pottery, sculpture, weaving, clubs, galleries, exhibitions - for increasing the interest of the girls, and inclusively catholic in her definition of art, so that no girl need think that she was incapable of expressing herself through this medium. Her approach was often unconventional; on one occasion nude self-portraits of the Art Sixth, drawn while lying in their baths, were exhibited around the school for all to admire! But then, this was a woman who bathed *au naturel* on Dartmoor, and had turned down proposals of marriage from three different suitors, all of them clergymen!

On the School Birthday, 1953, all was ready for the formal opening of the new house. The Bishop of Kensington officiated. First he unveiled the carved wooden tablet (in Room 3) renaming the house "Moberly Bell House", then, in a procession which included MB, Miss Lupton, and Miss Marshall, he solemnly blessed every room in the building and dedicated the house to its new purpose. Once more, the School had room to breathe and grow, and the dark days of "make-do and mend" and war-time austerity seemed to have receded. The School, too, now had a permanent memorial to its founder.

> *"On this Michaelmas Day it is our joy and privilege to celebrate the incorporation of a third house into the School building, the gift of the London Diocesan Board of Education.*
>
> *"And since it is not bricks and mortar alone which constitute a school, it is the wish of the Governors, Headmistress and Staff that this extension should forever be associated with the name of Miss Moberly Bell, who, as founder, benefactor and first Headmistress, gave so generously of herself to the School. In token of the honour in which we hold her we, therefore, rename this house Moberly Bell House.*
>
> *"And, that each succeeding generation of girls may remember her to whom we owe so much, I unveil this Tablet, placed here by her former colleagues."*
>
> (Magazine 31, 1952-53)

Building the New Assembly Hall.

Bricks and mortar

The acquisition of Henniker House now made it possible for all of MB's grandiose schemes for Assembly Hall and Gymnasium to go ahead; at least the space to build them was available. All that was now needed was time, money, and a good firm of architects. It was to be another twelve years before all was complete. Meanwhile, constantly surrounded by workmen and their materials, Lady Margaret got on with the business of being a School.

The School Magazines during those twelve years give a picture of the usual purposeful activity that was typical of a grammar school in those days. There was little television, nor many of the other distractions of modern childhood, and much of one's youthful enthusiasm was expended at school. Drama continued to be a strong tradition, despite the manifest inadequacies of the old Hall and its stage. There was yet another production of *Hansel and Gretel*, directed by Miss Console, an accomplished musician as well as French teacher, at Christmas 1954; and the following summer a memorable performance of *Twelfth Night*, during which Caitlin Hughes's tights split! The years that followed saw *Eager Heart* (a Christmas morality play), Shaw's *Androcles and the Lion*, a Nativity play, *Away in a Manger*, another Shaw, *St Joan*, *The Snow Queen* (Christmas 1958), and an uproarious Staff Pantomime, *Victoriella*, in which Parson Green and his two daughters, Bethnal and Golders, crossed swords with a tough policeman, PC "Hammer" Smith. Christopher Fry's *A Boy with a Cart*, telling the story of St Cuthman of Wessex, in July 1963, was the first play performed in the new Assembly Hall, possession of which had been taken on All Saints' Day, 1962.

School journeys flourished - Stratford (1954), Switzerland (1956, 1959, 1963), Paris (1957), Derbyshire (1958), Italy and Denmark (1960), Holland and Provence (1961), and Spain (1963). A variety of School Clubs sprang up, some short-lived, as enthusiasms came and went, and others proving more lastingly popular. Miss Boundy had seen to it that there were both senior and junior Art Clubs, each with its own activities and programme of visits. A Music Club was formed, which periodically listened to gramophone records and then discussed them. The Theatre Club (1954) held frequent play-readings, and organised visits to productions locally and in town. The Debating Society (1955) gave a generation of LMS girls the chance to exercise their arguing skills. An Opera Club (1958) and a Miscellany Society (1957) - the latter devoted to a variety of pass-times, as its name suggests - came and went. The Aletheia Society (1956) was a rather more serious affair altogether, and a more permanent one; its name is the Greek word for truth, and its members held philosophical and religious discussions in their search for it. The Science Club and Photography Club are self-explanatory. The Hiking Club organised week-end tramps about the countryside, while the Garden Club (1959) sought to make the area around the Chapel (then, it will be remembered, in the garden where the Geography Room now is) as beautiful as possible.

One institution set up by Miss Marshall was the series of Commemoration Day lectures. In her quest for ways to broaden the horizons of her senior girls, eminent persons were invited along to talk to the Governors, Staff, parents, and the Fifth and Sixth Forms on or around March 18th, as a way of marking this particular date in the School Calendar. The School had no tradition of Speech Days, as had Whitelands, but this, it was felt, could fill that hole. The first speaker, in 1958, was Lady Cynthia Colville, for many years Lady-in-Waiting to Queen Mary, a social worker and magistrate; she gave her audience a vivid insight into various aspects of her work. In 1959, Mr Michael Stewart, MP for Fulham, spoke on the development of government in Britain. Flora Robson, the actress, came in 1960, to speak on "Ambition". Miss Mary Stocks (later Baroness Stocks) (1961) spoke on the increasing role of women in society, and the Bishop of London, the Rt Rev Robert Stopford (who as Canon Stopford had once been a Governor of the School) (1962) spoke on "Responsibility".

The younger ones, too, had their visiting lecturers - George Cansdale on "Animals of West Africa" (he brought with him Polly the Bush Baby and Percy the Python!), a Miss Wood from the Cherry Marshall Agency on "Dress and Grooming", Rex Harris on Jazz, and Noel Streatfeild on books, to name but a few.

Highlights of those twelve years are many. Miss Boundy organised a very instructive Greek Exhibition in March 1954, in order to open the girls' eyes to the influence of Greek thought, art, and culture on our present civilisation. A Spanish Market raised money to fulfil another ambition of Miss Boundy's - to have around the school good examples of modern-day art; the proceeds of the event went towards commissioning a

"Mother and Child", by Willi Soukop.

The School in 1965.

The gardens in 1965.

The new Assembly Hall, 1965.

The new Library, 1965.

sculpture from Mr Willi Soukop, "Mother and Child". It was finished by February 1957, and brought to the school amidst great excitement; there it was photographed, admired, and commented upon, before going off to be exhibited at the Royal Academy; it returned to the School permanently for the Birthday later that year, and now stands on the terrace outside the Hall. Later, a decision was made to sell the old piano given by Sir Valentine Chirol, and use the money to buy some modern paintings; Miss Boundy was a friend of John Piper (who died earlier this year), and she drove down to his home, a delightful farmhouse near Henley, with three of the Sixth Form, to collect her "loot".

> *We arrived without mishap and were met by John Piper and his wife Myfanwy, who is famous for her libretto for Benjamin Britten's opera "The Turn of the Screw" (for which John Piper did the decor).*
>
> *From the beginning they were very friendly and unassuming, so all our apprehensions disappeared. His studio is a converted barn with whitewashed brick walls. We spent the first hour browsing through his sketches and paintings, then selecting the ones we liked best. Eventually we narrowed the choice down to four paintings in "gouache" and one in oils. Our resources being limited, we were not able to afford a painting in oils, so instead we chose two gouache paintings, which we now have hanging in the main entrance hall of the School.* (Magazine 1964-65)

(They are still there, but have been moved up to the first floor landing, outside the Chapel.) Miss Boundy's unstinting hard work for the School over many years was rewarded when she was granted a Goldsmiths' Travelling Scholarship in 1963 for six months to travel and study among the art treasures of Italy.

Two big events of this period were the School's 40th, and MB's 80th, Birthdays. The Bishop of London preached at the Foundation Day Service at All Saints', Fulham, and afterwards, at a reception at the school, the former entrance through Belfield was opened up, so that guests could arrive in nostalgic style, each one announced in ringing tones by Mr Edwards. The September Birthday saw the formal acceptance of Mr Soukop's "Mother and Child". MB's birthday happened just as her dreams approached realisation; the LCC had approved the building of the new Hall, and an artist's impression of it was printed in the 1960-61 Magazine alongside the many tributes paid to her. She was honoured by an article in the family newspaper, The Times, on March 24th, 1961, devoted entirely to her life and achievements. On the morning itself the Head Girl and Deputy, with two of the First Form, called at her Chelsea home with good wishes and flowers; then

> *...in the evening the Old Girls gave a delightful party. There were so many people present that the necessity of our new hall was made even more apparent to us. Miss Lupton accompanied Miss Bell and Miss Marshall on to the platform at the beginning of the party, and Miss Bell cut her Birthday Cake. Then Diana Gunn (Mrs Glover) presented Miss Bell with a cheque for eighty guineas from the Old Girls and Friends of the school.* (Magazine 1960-61)

There were speeches by the current Head Girl, Barbara Miller, and the very first, Hazel Russell, who had been one of that pioneer group who had followed MB from Whitelands to the unknown fastnesses of Parson's Green. Characteristically, MB gave the money she had received towards a gift for the School. "I have written to the architect asking him to think of the best way to spend the money. I wonder if a representation of St Michael might be a good idea?" (Magazine 1960-61) When the new Hall was formally opened on 1965, there was indeed a St Michael guarding the entrance, the work of Stephen Sykes.

"The Opening of the New Buildings of Lady Margaret School", by HRH the Princess Alexandra of Kent, on 24th February 1965, marked the completion of years of seemingly non-stop work on the school site since its return from Midhurst in 1943. Moberly Bell House had been completely refurbished, passageways in all three houses had now been made on every floor (a great convenience, especially in wet weather), the new Hall had been finished, and the old Hall rebuilt as the present Gymnasium, Sir Valentine's two classrooms being converted into changing-room and showers. The School had been fortunate in securing the firm of Seely and Paget as architects, and Hussey Brothers as builders, and the whole work had been carried out with a sympathetic eye to the integrity of the old buildings (while making the new ones thoroughly modern and up-to-date) and remarkably little friction with a working school. One great sadness was that Lord Mottistone (formerly Mr Seely) had died before he could witness the ceremony marking the completion of his work on the School.

In her greeting to Princess Alexandra, Miss Marshall recalled that first Royal Visitor, Princess Marie Louise, way back in 1917, and MB's words that "there were many schools more famous than this but none that called forth more kindness and generosity". She even found words of thanks for the LCC, soon to be transformed into the Inner London Education Authority (ILEA), who had found it possible after all to sanction and partly finance the project. As the Princess toured the school, the shade of Pixie Ward must surely have been present!

Princess Alexandra talking with Willi Soukop, February 24th 1965.

> *When the Princess made her way out of the hall [wrote 12-year-old Amanda Hayes afterwards], those of us in the gymnasium got up and did some sequences and warming-up exercises to show the parents who were there. We suddenly caught a glimpse of the Princess coming through the gym door. All hearts turned over as Press photographers turned their cameras to the door through which the Princess appeared. A faint ray of sunshine came through the windows. We stood scared, excited and stiff as though we had been entranced by a spell. The cameras clicked; chairs were given to the Princess and Miss Marshall, and they sat down.*
>
> *We then got into our groups. The children who described the dances did very well, although they were nervous. The dances went very well. We all were happy that no one forgot anything.*   (Magazine, 1964-65)

The 50th Birthday celebrations were held on March 17th, 1967. In the morning, the School, all together in the new Assembly Hall, were addressed by Hazel Russell, the first Head Girl, and then a recorded message from MB herself was played to them. It was to be almost her last public appearence, so to speak, and perhaps she knew that, for she spoke from her heart. One is never alone in a job, she said, and she had had the blessing of a great many people in this her life's work. But though one is only one of many, each has his own important part to play; "you have your own unique job to do, and it is meant to be done by you in your way". Then, if one is sure that it is a good job to be doing, one is bound to succeed. Finally, with a side-swipe at the moves then being made by the authorities to change the pattern of education in London, about which she was scathing to the end, she said:

Princess Alexandra with Miss Marshall, February 24th 1965.

> *Then there is just one more thing. Anyone who has been in this School has been privileged. We hear a lot about privilege nowadays, always represented as something rather wicked and disgraceful and to be ashamed of. Now this is nonsense. You are privileged because you had enough brain to get into this kind of school. You came from a good and loving family that wanted you to have this kind of education....You have been privileged, you have had everything given to you, you had no right to them; there is nothing disgraceful in that. It is just as it happened. The only thing that matters is that, recognizing the fact that you are privileged, you also recognize the fact that therefore you owe a debt to society. Freely you have received, freely give.*   (Magazine, 1966-67)

Miss Marshall, MB, and Adrienne Hill (Head Girl), 50th Birthday 1967.

Then Hazel Russell and her latest successor, Adrienne Hill, planted a willow in the garden. The whole School was dismissed for the afternoon; and later, in the evening, they reassembled for the Jubilee Thanksgiving Service in Westminster Abbey, with the sermon by the Bishop of Peterborough, formerly Bishop of Kensington and Chairman of the Governors. At the reception that followed back at the school (a fleet of buses were hired for the occasion), the Parents' Association presented the School with a portrait of Miss Marshall, by Helen Lessore; MB was there, and made her very last speech. Less than a month later she was dead.

The Royal Visit of 1965, and the Golden Jubilee celebrations of 1967, aptly close a chapter in the history of the School. This vision of a finished task, that had been with MB since the 1920s, and which she had handed on to Miss Marshall to complete, had taken all her life to come to pass, but she had lived to see it fulfilled. Frail, almost blind, she nevertheless was still the indomitable Enid that had refused to bow to the inevitable fifty years earlier, and in her latter days found no difficulty in delivering a speech to a large gathering for an hour without notes. She died on April 13th, 1967. Her lifelong friend and companion, Miss Lupton, who had been with her throughout her life's work, did not survive the year, dying on December 2nd.

> *"I have said my Nunc Dimittis: the children are within the Covenant."*

Alarums and excursions

The Plan for London's education following the Second World War envisaged a comprehensive secondary school system; this, it was felt, was the only sure way to achieve the "parity of esteem" that the 1944 Act had piously wished. Ideally, the LCC would have liked a neat chequerboard of largish schools across the capital, each catering for the educational needs of all the children within its "catchment area". Had Hitler been more thorough in his bombing, this might have been a possibility. As it was, London had a large number of schools, of different ages, sizes, social mix, tradition, and reputation; and for many years to come it was going to have to make do with the buildings it had. It built enough new schools over the next twenty years catering for the "bulge" in the birth-rate, without providing perfectly sound buildings with purpose-built replacements.

The "county complementary" was one idea for making the best of what they had; Lady Margaret, as we have seen, was linked in this way with Hurlingham School, then in Hugon Road, but, apart from a few joint enterprises, such as a junior choir, nothing much in practice was made of this link. With hindsight, it perhaps was a pity that more effort was not put into making this initiative a success, for at least the LCC was not displaying that dogmatic rigidity of thinking which later came to characterise it and its successor, the ILEA. One suspects, however, that the later breed of local politician would have repudiated the complementary system out of hand, no matter how smoothly it was operating, as not fulfilling his own narrow criteria of what "comprehensive" meant.

In 1964, the "thirteen years of Tory misrule" came to an end, and Harold Wilson's Labour government took charge at Westminster. When that government was just eight months old, the Education Secretary, Mr Antony Crosland, issued (July 12th, 1965) the notorious Circular 10/65, *The Organisation of Secondary Education*, in which he "requested" local authorities to submit plans, within a suggested twelve months' deadline, for the reorganisation of their secondary schools so as to eliminate selection at the age of eleven. He had originally meant to "require" such plans, but it was pointed out to him that he did not have the legal authority to do so, not without a lengthy, and chancy, Bill through Parliament.

As a result of this circular, and of Circular 10/66 that followed it (in which the DES, possibly illegally, threatened to withhold finance for rebuilding from any authority that did not comply with the previous circular) the Deputy Education Officer of the ILEA, Dr Eric Briault, prepared a report for a meeting of the Schools Planning Sub-Committee in September 1966. This was the result of extensive consultations with the Aided Church schools of London. Lady Margaret's position was made plain from the start; it wished to remain a girls' school, it wished to keep its present site, it wished not to be a very large school (the Governors had already, in July 1963, agreed in principle to becoming a three-form entry school). Its conclusion was that it could not for the foreseeable future be other than it was at the moment. Nevertheless, by the following June, a note of resignation in the face of the inevitable was apparent.

> *The Chairman said he had had an interview with Dr Briault, and felt that as we have a government which is committed to comprehensive education, we are not in a position to resist, because we are dependent on the state for most of our money, and no support will be forthcoming from the state if we hold a policy contrary to theirs. Within this position, however, we should work to get the best possible future for the girls and the school.*
>
> (Minutes, June 9th, 1966)

Nevertheless, the Governors reiterated their determination to remain single-sex, and on their present site. They did suggest that, if the clinic buildings next door to Moberly Bell House could be acquired, they would consider becoming a seven-form entry comprehensive! A non-selective school had to be that large, it was then believed, to generate a Sixth Form of a reasonable size. Even Miss Marshall was of this view:

> *...a comprehensive school needed to be larger than 5 f.e. to produce a viable VI Form. The VI Form was not separable from the rest of the School; integration spread lower down the School, and in a joint VI form problems of loyalty could arise.*
>
> (Minutes, Jan.30th, 1967)

The proposals eventually put forward in Dr Briault's report were that Lady Margaret and St Mark's should each be a single-sex, six-form entry school, with a joint mixed Sixth Form on the Lady Margaret site; expansion for Lady Margaret could be achieved

68

by the use of the Ackmar Road School premises. Neither school was entirely happy with this plan, especially not St Mark's, who preferred expanding on their own into a six-form entry mixed school. An alternative plan, whereby St Mark's, as an 11-14 boys' school, and a Lady Margaret junior school housed in the Ackmar Road buildings, also 11-14, would "feed" a mixed 14-18 school in the main Lady Margaret buildings, also met with little approval. The nature of the proposals, despite Dr Briault's best endeavours in trying to sell them to the Governors, made Lady Margaret determined to have nothing to do with them.

> *After a great deal of discussion, the Governors agreed that this was not the moment to make a decision about the future of the School. They felt that there is an excellent educational unit here which is supported by Governors, staff, and parents, and they do not wish this to be upset until it is clear that there is a better educational alternative.*
>
> *(Minutes, Jan.30th, 1967)*

A typically trenchant comment was vouchsafed by MB to the local press only a fortnight before she died.

> *"If the NUT and all the other idiots get their way and make everything merge into comprehensive schools then of course there will be no education left. I don't think comprehensive schools need always be wrong; it sounds the right thing for a place like Anglesey. But our Governors are refusing to back it because they can't see that it will help a single child.*
>
> *"You can't even say our school preserves class distinctions. We had a grand-daughter of the Bishop of London and daughters of professional people along with children in care of the LCC and children of policemen and busmen." (Fulham Chronicle, Apr.6th, 1967)*

Dr Briault's plans were subsequently withdrawn, and the Headmistress was able to report that applications for the sixty First Form places for September 1967 had soared to a hundred.

Meanwhile, one of the Governors, Dr Cameron, came up with a novel suggestion - that the School investigate the possibility that it might become a specialist school, catering particularly for dyslexics. The idea of "teaching centres", he thought, could be extended; schools could specialise in one of the three sciences, for example, and neighbouring schools in the others, and Advanced level pupils could take their specialist training in each; the same idea could be applied to modern languages. A sub-committee was formed, and the initiative thoroughly chewed over, but eventually it was considered inappropriate for Lady Margaret, dedicated as it was to turning out "whole persons", as another Governor put it.

The School's expanding to three forms of entry was a possibility, however. The London Diocesan Board of Education were keen on the idea. But the blessing of the DES, which the School would require, would hardly be forthcoming in the circumstances. Even so, the much increased Sixth Form, and the need for better Staff accommodation, once again made more space desirable; the clinic next door became vacant, and moves were set in train to acquire it. A desultory period of suggestion, offers, correspondence, hardly negotiation, took place over the next few years, but nothing came of it.

Then, at the Labour Party Conference at Blackpool in 1968, Miss Alice Bacon, Minister of State at the DES, announced that the Government would introduce a Bill to compel local authorities to reorganise on comprehensive lines. A Bill was brought in to give effect to this pledge in the autumn of 1969, but before it had completed all its stages through Parliament, the Labour Government had been defeated at the General Election of June 1970, and a Conservative administration had taken its place.

Miss Marshall took advantage of the lull in the fighting to announce her retirement. It was 1971, and she had, it seemed, been hard at it since 1947 without respite - building, expanding, defending the integrity of the School. She was not entirely well, either, and would be glad to lay down the cudgels for a while. She saw too that the fight was not over, and that a younger, fresher general might be better for leading whatever offensive or defensive actions the future might bring. She was also 60 years old, a good age to go, since she was still young enough to pursue other interests. This she did, becoming Chairman of Whitelands College Council, of which she had long been a member, and as such a prime mover in the formation of the Roehampton Institute of Higher Education, a federation of four Colleges - including Whitelands - in the Wimbledon area; this reorganisation allowed for the expansion of what had been just teacher-training establishments into a much broadened academic institution of university standard.

To Elsie Marshall must go the credit for making of Lady Margaret a school of high academic repute. MB had always thought of it as "her school", and indeed it was; but the cosiness of the relationship had masked to some degree the fact that, in terms of academic achievement, though it had its periodic successes, it was some way from the top of the list. When Miss Marshall came (from a school that really did achieve academically) perhaps one or two girls a year would go on to university; comparatively few girls remained at school long enough to try. Miss Marshall changed all that. Girls were encouraged to remain at school - beyond 15, beyond the Fifth Form. The Sixth Form grew from a score to a century, and more, and its members were encouraged to aim high. That was her supreme achievement; the image that the School now has of itself, and presents to the outside world, was her doing. It was still "the particularly happy place" that MB had called into being; but "Flo" (as the girls somewhat irreverently called her behind her back) had made it something more.

"The Beggar's Opera", July 1965.

The latter years of Miss Marshall's headship, despite the on-going battles with the local authority, were ones of solid advancement. With the facilities provided by the new Hall (the two classrooms behind the stage had always been intended to double as "green rooms"), there was a flourishing of school drama. The 1964 Shakespeare Quatercentenary was the occasion for a team of Staff - Miss Masaroon on the production, Miss Console and Mrs Hogg (the Music Mistress) on the musical embellishments, Mrs Burt (of the PE staff) on the dancing, and Miss Boundy on the sets - to stage a production of *Much Ado About Nothing*. But it was with the appointment of the School's first full-time drama teacher, Peter Miles, that the "school play" became quasi-professional theatre. Each summer, after the examinations, until he left in 1968 (having married the Classics mistress), Mr Miles worked his magic. In 1965, Gay's *The Beggar's Opera*, in 1966, Shakespeare's *The Taming of the Shrew*, in 1967, Gordon Daviot's *Dickon*, and in 1968, Benn Levy's *The Rape of the Belt*, rang the changes and made demands on their young performers that Peter Miles ensured were met with total success. His successor, Nick Ruscoe, had a very different approach; a performance entitled *Moving Through*, in 1970, in which girls recited psyche-searching free verse of their own composition from the tops of step-ladders, and variously displayed the nuclear *Angst* of the modern generation, was politely rather than enthusiastically received. It certainly provoked a great deal of discussion, along the lines of "What was all that about?"

"The Taming of the Shrew", July 1967.

Cultural life blossomed. In an inter-house drama competition in 1964, and in a similar music competition in 1966, Carver showed its superiority in the arts; the novelist Margaret Drabble visited the school to talk about her work; Mrs Hogg's husband, the actor Ian Hogg (who played Macduff in the film version of *Macbeth*) came to read poetry to the Fifth Form; Miss Boundy organised an art educational trip to Italy. School journeys to Burgundy, Norway, and Austria were arranged and enjoyed. For the first time in the School's history, a professional librarian was appointed to the Staff, Mrs Diana Purcell. (She is, at the time of writing, still in harness, having received glowing tributes recently from Her Majesty's Inspectors on her role within the School.) The concern that the School had long had for social problems (back in the 1930s they helped Miss Lupton at the Housing Centre) led to the forming of the Social Services Committee, run by the Sixth Form, to coordinate the School's charitable work. Every Christmas, the Fourth Forms made it their special task to entertain the children of the school for the deaf in Ackmar Road with food, games, and presents. The Sixth Form grew and grew, and successes at "A" level and entries to universities went up and up. (One of the successful candidates, in 1965, was Janet Bull - Art, English, History - who married a Mr Street-Porter and made a name for herself in the media.) And, in an interesting experiment which would certainly now be illegal, Miss Marshall in 1969, following a spate of young marrieds and pregnancies among her Staff, and wishing to achieve some stability among her work-force, appointed an unusually large number of men (among whom was the present writer), much to the delight of the girls!

When Miss Marshall left, there were tributes in the Magazine from past and present Chairmen of Governors - the Bishop of Peterborough and Ronald Goodchild, Bishop of Kensington; from past and present Staff - Miss Long (the Deputy Headmistress), Miss Masaroon, Miss Aldrick, Miss Millington; from past Head Girls - Barbara Miller and Molly Adams (Mrs Lawrence). The day after Foundation Day, Friday March 19th, the Old Girls and Parents packed the Hall to bid her farewell; the following day nearly 90 Staff, past and present, paid their respects; and on her very last day, March 31st, the School followed suit.

> *All were glad that, as she spoke, the Assembly Hall and the gardens beyond the windows, for which she was so much responsible, beamed back at her, gracious and comely in the spring sunshine.*
> (*Magazine, 1970-71*)

Battle lost - and won

Alison Cavendish

The School's third Headmistress was Miss Alison Cavendish, lately Deputy Headmistress at Grey Coat Hospital. She came from the West Country, the daughter of a clergyman, and sister of Richard Cavendish, the publisher. She had been a pupil at Bath High School, and from there won an entrance scholarship to the Royal Holloway College, London. After graduating, she spent two more years researching for her MA, then embarked on a career in librarianship. After a year at the National Central Library, she changed course, and trained as a teacher. Upon qualifying, she held a post as History mistress at Sydenham High School for eight years, before being appointed to Grey Coat. Her outwardly shy and unassertive demeanour was deceptive; the next eight years, during which she steered, with cool unflappability, a seemingly frail vessel through some ferocious tempests, were to demonstrate for the third time in the School's history that the right woman always turns up when her particular talents are most needed.

The new Government did not call a halt to the comprehensive process, and local authorities were at liberty to proceed with whatever plans they had. But what the new Education Secretary, Mrs Margaret Thatcher, was not prepared to sanction was the sort of botched proposal that several authorities had been putting forward in their anxiety to change. Schools which felt that their authority's proposals were damaging to the educational interests of their pupils had the right of appeal to the Secretary of State in the last resort.

The ILEA's new ideas were set out in a review of Secondary Provision, issued on July 21st, 1972. These were discussed, and issued a year later in a document entitled *Planning for 1980* (proof, if proof were needed, of the forward-looking nature of ILEA policy!). The Authority was of the opinion that there were too many single-sex schools in London, and too many Church schools as well; that they seemed to be popular with parents, for a variety of reasons, of which sex and religion were only a couple, was neither here nor there. The ILEA acquired an unexpected ally in this train of thought in the London and Southwark Diocesan Boards of Education, which expressed themselves in agreement with the ILEA that there was "a disproportionate number of single-sex schools in the ILEA area", and welcomed the "opportunity to reduce the number of our secondary schools" (Church of England Secondary Schools in Inner London: a Review - Jan.1973). From this point on, the School felt that it had two forces to contend with in its struggle, and Prebendary Tinker, the London Board's emissary, became something of an *eminence grise* in the fevered, but historically informed, imagination of Miss Cavendish.

The latest plan for Lady Margaret was that the School should become part of a 1200-strong mixed comprehensive, by amalgamating either with St Mark's and Grey Coat, or with St Mark's and Burlington; in either case the new school would not be at Parson's Green. The Governors, and even more so the Parents, could hardly give it credence. The proposal ignored completely the wishes and desires of the combining schools, overlooked entirely their separate traditions and histories, set aside totally the expressed preferences of parents and children. The detailed plan dealt solely in "form-bases" and "projected numbers", statistics which have proved in practice to have been imports from Fairyland!

Both sides were aired in the local press - the Authority:

> "By having bigger schools, the pupils will have a wider range of subjects available to them, because the school will be able to employ more teaching staff," said a spokesman for the ILEA.
> "In a small school you have a small staff where some of the teachers may have to teach more than one subject, and yet the pupils are trying to secure competitive public examinations. In a bigger school, because there is a bigger staff, the teachers can be more specialised." (Fulham Chronicle, Jan.19th, 1973)

and the School (or rather the Parents, through the Secretary of the Action Committee, formed to defend the integrity of the School):

> "Any caring parent," said Mr Michael Hildred, "knows the ideal school should be small enough to retain a certain ethos, to be able to have an approachable head and staff.
> "Over-large schools seem to have brought out all the worst features of city life. Apart from the fact that small grammar schools have a proven record of scholastic results, achieved over many years, while the comprehensives with thousands of children have a rather sorry record to date," continued Mr Hildred.

"Once the bulldozers have done what even Hitler never achieved, the parents with children attending primary schools will have no choice left but to send their children to these educational bureaucracies known as comprehensive schools," said Mr Hildred indignantly. (Fulham Chronicle, Jan.19th, 1973)

Mike Hildred, with two daughters in the school, and an hotelier in his spare time, put his business and organisational acumen at the service of the School. A high-profile car-sticker campaign had a "Save Lady Margaret School" slogan being touted as far off as Rome!

The School's counter-proposal, if indeed change was unavoidable, was for an expansion of Lady Margaret, on its own site, to a comprehensive school of three, or at the most five, forms of entry; in this way, the School would not lose its identity, and it could perhaps retain much of its prevailing ethos. But this was hardly to the liking of the ILEA; it was a reduction in the number of Church School places they were seeking, not an increase.

It was at this stage of proceedings that the School bade farewell to Miss Long. Katherine Long, a Cambridge graduate, was the School's first "permanent" Deputy Headmistress (before that, senior staff took it in turns to spend three years in the job). Like Miss Cavendish, she was an historian, and had come from Grey Coat, and during her hectic nine years had seen the completion of the extensive building programme, with all the chaos that such things bring to a Deputy Head, and the anxiety brought about by the series of proposals for the School's future. Her oft-expressed wish, that just for once she might have a quiet, uneventful term, was never granted. She exercised authority sweetly and mildly; one did things that she asked because one felt such a worm when she heaved a sigh and murmured: "Well, never mind. I'll see if I have time to do it." There was a record number of applicants for her post; eventually, the Governors picked upon yet another historian, from Camden School for Girls, Mrs Joan Olivier.

Prebendary Tinker, of the Diocesan Board, was quite anxious that Lady Margaret should think seriously about moving from the ILEA area to the outer London suburbs, where there was a comparative scarcity of Church places; this the Governors rejected at their meeting of June 21st, and decided instead to explore the possibility of joining with Grey Coat on the site of the College of St Mark and St John, in the King's Road. But there were other plans for the College, and that plan foundered.

By the end of the year, the ILEA were clearly becoming exasperated with this trouble-some school in their midst. In their review of Secondary School Provision in North and North-West London, presented to the Development Sub-Committee on December 11th, 1973, they proposed, rather curtly:

i. *Consultations authorized with the London Diocesan Board of Education and the governors on*
    a) *possibilities for the development of the school outside the Authority's area or*
    b) *amalgamation with St Mark's, in buildings to be determined, as a 750-place mixed CE comprehensive school, and*
ii. *the Governors to be informed that in the event of no practical proposal for inclusion in the comprehensive system being acceptable to them, the Authority may consider that the future of the school should lie outside the maintained sector of secondary education as far as Inner London is concerned.*

It must be said that St Mark's were no more happy with this proposal than Lady Margaret was. Mr Braide, the Senior Assistant Education Officer of the ILEA, attended a Governor's meeting on June 20th, 1974, to put the Authority's case once more, as persuasively as he could. By this time, the political scene had changed; the Conservative Government was out, and Mr Wilson was again Prime Minister; those who were determined on a comprehensive system were in the ascendant. The Governors answered as best they could: they had explored all the possibilities put forward by Mr Braide, and none of them met the grave reservations expressed by Governors, Staff, or Parents.

In desperation, at their meeting on November 7th, the Governors resurrected Professor Cameron's proposal, that the School should seek to be a specialist centre, for dyslexia, for example; and when Peter Newsam, of the ILEA, asked for a decision by November 13th, the Governors tentatively put the idea forward, as well as agreeing to explore forms of cooperation with other schools in a comprehensive partnership. There was even the possibility that Lady Margaret should once more become an independent school, and Mr Sell, Chairman of the Parents' Association, sent a questionnaire to all parents asking if they would be willing to pay fees for their daughters. An emissary from Emmanuel School, at Battersea, tried to talk the Staff into supporting such a change, which his school was set upon doing; but the Staff were not persuaded. Miss Cavendish had some preliminary discussions with Miss Dean, the Headmistress of Goldolphin and Latymer, on the suggestion that they might together form a 5-form-entry comprehensive school.

There was a further development at the next meeting of the Governors, on February 11th, 1975. There were two new ILEA Governors present for the first time, Anne Sofer and Tyrrell Burgess, the latter a well-known writer on educational matters, and both keen supporters of the comprehensive ideal. Perhaps the Governors were by now becoming paranoid, but several of them were of the mind that the two new members were in some sense Trojan horses, or "moles", as John Le Carre would say, whose function it was to ensure in some arcane manner that the Governors rapidly arrived at the Authority's desired end. Be that as it may (and Mr Burgess has always denied it), their conversion to Social Democracy some years later was an indication that here were two minds rather than two mouthpieces. It was Tyrrell Burgess who, at his first meeting as a Governor, set in train a new line of thinking that was to prove the salvation of the School.

> *Mr Burgess then suggested that it was possible that the ILEA would be sympathetic to a proposal that Lady Margaret School should retain its present identity on its existing site if the Governors express the intention of working towards non-selection by a stated date.* (Minutes, Feb.11th, 1975)

It was agreed that Miss Cavendish and the Staff would explore the feasibility of the School's becoming non-selective while remaining its present size. Prebendary Tinker, meanwhile, Rector no doubt of the parish of Nephelococcygia, continued to press for amalgamation with St Mark's.

A small working party of the staff (the Headmistress, Mrs Olivier, Miss Andrew, Mrs Fraser, and Mrs Skewes) was set up to carry out the feasibility study; part of this entailed visits to existing small comprehensive schools in the West Country and Yorkshire to see what lessons might be drawn and whether they might be applied to Lady Margaret. A letter was dispatched to the ILEA, informing them of the Governors' actions, and giving an assurance that the feasibility study would be completed by the next Governors' meeting, on July 8th. Dr Briault's reply, on May 15th, expressed the Authority's willingness to await the outcome of the study. His report to the Development Sub-Committee, while stressing the ILEA's (and the Diocesan Board's) preference for an amalgamation with St Mark's, indicated their willingness to consider the School's alternative proposal when it came; cooperation at Sixth Form and upper school level was promised by St Mark's, anxious to do anything that would preserve their identity.

Fact-finding missions were sent to Devizes and Kirkby Lonsdale, to look at small schools actually in operation. A visit to Dauntsey's School at Devizes saw cooperation at Sixth Form level in a remarkable form, for Dauntsey's, an independent school, provided much of the "A" level teaching, free of charge, for pupils of the local maintained comprehensive school. Existing cooperation was examined; for some time the School had sent girls to Hammersmith and West London College for "A" level Economics, and there were various informal links with Burlington and Hurlingham. (This was nothing new, in fact. When Margaret Ironside announced her intention, in 1923, of reading Mathematics at Cambridge, it was arranged that she should do applied maths at Fulham County and physics at Chelsea Polytechnic). The disadvantages of being small, largely those of the breadth of the curriculum, were acknowledged; but by cooperation with other institutions, and by a degree of flexibility in the organisation of classes, many of these problems could be overcome. The advantages, on the other hand, had not been given enough weight. A small school environment, it was argued, had far fewer of the disciplinary and social problems seemingly inherent in a larger school; children were more involved, and had each to bear a greater share of responsibility; there was a more intimate ethos, a less oppressive bureaucracy, easier communication.

> *It seems that most small secondary schools are in rural rather than urban areas. But the social strengths they show have particular relevance in an urban setting where social patterns, housing, etc., often conspire against a sense of personal importance for the teenager.* (Feasibility Study, June 1975)

There was great disappointment among some of the parents, who had campaigned hard and long to keep the School as it was. But most of them saw reality when it stared them in the face, and it now seemed possible that the School would at least preserve its existence, something which Miss Cavendish in her darkest hours had thought less and less likely, as she later admitted. Dr Briault had already informed the school that

> ...*the Authority declares its intention to submit proposals to cease to maintain any voluntary school whose governors have not given their agreement by the end of the summer term 1975 ...* (Letter to Clerk to Governors, May 15th, 1975)

On September 25th the Development Sub-Committee approved the scheme. Instantly, money was forthcoming to provide facilities to accommodate the new intake, and work was put in hand to build the latest in Home Economics Rooms on top of the History and Geography Rooms. Offers of cooperation came in, or were sought, from neighbouring schools, including St Mark's and Fulham Gilliatt (now Fulham Cross). The School drew up a new admission agreement, and henceforth girls would be admitted according to the ILEA's "banding" formula, which ensured that each school got its "fair share" of pupils of differing abilities. The required Public Notice, advertising the School's change of status, was put out on January 14th, 1976; the School would receive its first all-ability intake in September 1977. The deed was done, and Lady Margaret was opening yet another chapter in its history.

Eucharist in the School Hall. The Rev. Dick Ashton is celebrant.

Ruth Hogg (Head Girl 1970) and contemporaries, in mini-skirts!

Comprehensive School

ithin three years of accepting the change in the School's status, Alison Cavendish, with much heart-searching, resigned, and accepted the Headship of Sutton High School. The arduous struggle to preserve the good thing she had found at Parson's Green had exhausted her. There was some degree of bitterness, too, for an Authority which dealt with people, and particularly with children, not on the basis of what they might want or what is their good, but what the Authority conceived to be in their interests, interpreted in a narrow, partisan, and arrogantly bureaucratic manner that scarcely brooked dissent. She was later to write:

> The plans for reorganisation promulgated by the ILEA - those for Division 1 being presented at a meeting by Dr Briault - were thought of by administrature in terms of buildings and numbers. (Natty plans showing up-to-date buildings in different colours, and numbers which could conveniently merge to make the orthodox size of comprehensive - 6-form-entry the usual minimum was then the orthodox view.) They betrayed little or no understanding of localities, traditions and people.
>
> Because of the County Hall emphasis on buildings, numbers and system, there seemed to be no willingness at the centre to recognise why it is that real parents with real children living in a particular part of the urban jungle choose schools. In general parents were not concerned with system or theory (or even subject choice beyond a certain point) but went to open days or open evenings to look at local schools.

What made the whole business worse was the clear impression of particular animosity felt by some at County Hall for all Aided schools. The degree of independence enjoyed by schools such as Lady Margaret meant in practice that the Authority's writ in several things stopped at the school gates; and this limitation on their powers was a hard thing to bear for people who considered they knew what was best in all circumstances for their fellow citizens. Some schools did not survive; Mary Datchelor, in Camberwell, a school very like Lady Margaret in size and ethos, closed down. Others, like Goldolphin and Latymer, opted for independence. Lady Margaret was adamant that it wanted to do neither; but in so doing, thinks Miss Cavendish it took a big gamble.

> I do think the survival of the School was touch and go. (Sometimes I used to lie awake, riven with anxiety, thinking that if we were forced to close I would organise the biggest party in creation, so that we would go out with a bang, not a whimper!)
>
> I think we survived for two reasons. Firstly, everyone connected with LMS had shown such unity, commitment, rationality and determination that probably ILEA felt it simplest to give way, and let us go comprehensive alone. Secondly, I suspect that ILEA felt we could not make a small comprehensive work in practice, so thought we would soon wither away.

While all this was going on, the School was getting about its usual business. The Sixth Form remained at 100+, and in the year that the first all-ability intake was admitted, 18 of those leaving went on to university, 13 others to further education of one kind or another, and the rest into employment (for some years the BBC seemed to be a favourite destination). Maria Soteriou (1966-73) was one of the pioneer six women admitted to Wadham College, Oxford, when it became a "mixed" college; she was responsible for a "fringe" production at the 1974 Edinburgh Festival, and after graduating took up a theatrical career. The Modern Languages department continued to win more than its fair share of Travel Scholarships. Spanish and Russian were added to the curriculum. And a new venture was the yearly French exchange, whereby the Third Forms would spend a week at Easter living *en famille* with a similarly aged class in a French school, and the following term the French children would reciprocate by coming to England, and attending classes at the school. Another new departure was the post-examination Fifth Form excursion; the entire year went off to spend a week in Liverpool (1973), Matlock (1974 and 1975), Bangor (1976), Yorkshire (1976) or Amsterdam (1977) in order to unwind and learn how to be Sixth Formers. Mrs Smith took music in the School to new heights; a record number of girls were learning instruments, and a series of major musical events - among them Pergolesi's *Stabat Mater* - put Lady Margaret on the musical map. Anne Walhouse (later Mrs Kennedy), the new junior in the English department, formed a Madrigal Group that was soon competing at Llangollen and winning a First Place certificate in the Brent Festival. There were the major dramatic productions - *Papageno* (an adaptation of *The Magic Flute*), produced by Miss Console shortly before she retired, *The Importance of Being Earnest*, *A Midsummer Night's Dream* (Puck was played by Miranda Foster, daughter of the actor Barry Foster - she later followed her father into an acting career), *Androcles and the Lion*, *Lady Precious Stream*, and, the crown of them all, Miss Miller's and Mrs Smith's production of Sandy Wilson's *The Boy Friend*.

> *The curtain went up on Kerry Duke's thighs, delightful objects in themselves, but coupled with her eyes and voice the very epitome of every jaded man's illusion of a French maid. Thereafter the delights followed effortlessly upon each other's heels. Even the champagne mysteriously turning to blood, and the waiter wobbling off with the giggles, for all the world like a blackcurrant jelly in an earth tremor, only added to their number.*
>
> *The school was more than fortunate to have taken into the first form the daughter of Terry Gilbert, who did the choreography for the Twiggy film. Mr Gilbert enthusiastically offered his services, and much of the professionalism of the final result must be attributed to him.* (Magazine, 1976-77)

A more light-hearted piece was the Staff Pantomime of 1976, *The Phantom Fiddler of Parson's Green*, when Mr Owen, as Harlequin, tied up the Headmistress (disguised as a policeman) with a string of sausages!

There was a major change to the composition of the Order in 1975. The numbers had been growing inexorably, with the increase of the Sixth Form, and by the mid-70s there were often forty members, with another fifteen or twenty on the Probation. It was decided, after consultation with the Sixth Form, that all Sixth Formers would be called on for various prefectorial duties, and they would be organised by a small executive committee of six, including the Head Girl and Deputy; these six only would enjoy the distinction of being "The Order".

In preparation for C-Day, the Staff betook themselves to a variety of courses so that they would be qualified to teach pupils less able than those they had been used to. For many of them, it was their introduction to the CSE (Certificate of Secondary Education, which had been set up to provide certification for those pupils for whom GCE "O" level was not appropriate; the two examinations were later merged as the GCSE). Miss Andrew, whose subject, Classics, would be disappearing in the new circumstances, retrained as a remedial teacher (or "Special Needs", as it came to be called). The English department attended a day's course in Chelsea, where they were lectured by old hands from the established comprehensive schools; they were told, in answer to their question "What reading books could be used in a mixed ability First Form class?", that there were lots. "Name three," the Head of English asked politely, whipping out a notebook and pencil. "Well," said the expert, "there's *Charley and the Chocolate Factory*." "They've mostly read that at primary school," murmured the H of E."Two more?" "Well, see me afterwards. I must get on now." Suffice it to say, another two were not forthcoming, and the English department, when the time came, taught by the seat of its collective pants, with no discernably awful results.

The new intake of September, 1977, did not, on the face of it, seem so very different from previous years. There were some girls who clearly would never have got into the school in its grammar school days, and who clearly were never going to do "O" level. But all of them had that shiny-eyed keenness that characterises Lady Margaret girls, at least in their first year or two in the school. It was also the School's 60th Birthday that month, and it was decided to speed the process of assimilation of the new intake by having each of the four houses (as the divisions were now generally called) organise and perform a short play in the afternoon of the Birthday. Strictly speaking, it was not a contest, but there was certainly a competitive edge to the proceedings. By the end of the day, the object of integration had certainly been achieved.

The Talent Competition, the 60th Birthday, 1977.

The grammar school intake was allowed to work itself out over the next six years, as each new all-ability intake arrived. The staff for the most part learned on the job. Evidently they did not do too badly; seventeen of them passed "A" level in 1984, one of them, Sophie McLaughlin, gaining a place at Christ Church, Oxford, to read English. (Sophie was also an accomplished artist, and produced the fine drawing of the school garden which has decorated so many of the School's publications, and was chosen to embellish the 75th Birthday Mug.)

When Miss Cavendish left, at the end of the Summer Term, 1980, she left behind her a School not so very different to the outward eye from the one she had inherited from Miss Marshall. The herculean task she had performed in maintaining the School's integrity and identity had taken its toll; and towards the end of her time at the school she had to endure a rather nasty throat operation. She was ready, while she was still young enough, to cruise on calmer seas. (While she was away, Mrs Fraser acted as Headmistress, since Mrs Olivier was off at the same time having James!)

The Governors appointed Mrs Rosemary Cairns, formerly Deputy Headmistress at Danemark School in Winchester, as the School's fourth Headmistress, and its first married one.

Winds of Change

Rosemary Cairns came at a time when the School was just beginning to feel "comprehensive". The all-ability intake had reached the Fourth Form when she took up the reins of office, and the last of the grammar school intake were embarking on their "O" level year. She herself had had experience of comprehensive school teaching and management, and these assets would be put to use in the years to follow. The educational scene had, of course, changed again, with the election of a Conservative government the year before; and a former Education secretary was now Prime Minister. The grocer's daughter from Grantham had fairly astringent views on the economy, learned, no doubt, in the hard school of her father's shop; and these principles, when applied to public sector pay, meant some degree of dissent from those affected by them. One group that felt strongly that its members were undervalued and underpaid was the teaching profession; and the scene was set for the wearisome alternation of strike and work-to-rule that would bedevil the schools over the next few years. Mrs Cairns had a great deal of sympathy for her staff in this conflict, but she also had a school to run; and friction at times was inevitable.

Rosemary Cairns

Mrs Cairns had studied French at Angers University, and then returned to England to read History at London. In a short period of study at Cambridge, she had acquired a fascination with linguistics. Her other great passion was music, which she shared with her husband, David Cairns, music critic of the Sunday Times. They also shared three sons.

She began her teaching career at Putney High School, and from there, by way of contrast, moved to Vauxhall Manor, in South London. She was later appointed Head of English at Barnes School, from where she spent a term at Cambridge on a Teachers' Fellowship, pursuing her interest in language. Subsequently she was appointed Deputy Head at Danemark School in Winchester, and it was from there that she came to Lady Margaret School.

Rosemary Cairns arrived just as the ILEA were beginning a major review of secondary provision throughout the Authority's area. Lady Margaret was immediately affected by this, because it was proposed that there should be a reduction of school rolls in Division 1 (Kensington and Chelsea, Hammersmith and Fulham) to reflect a projected fall in the child population. There was an angry response to this from the school; for the ILEA's preferred method of achieving this was to have every school reduce by the same percentage, so that none would be more disadvantaged than any other. Loss of pupils, of course, meant loss of teaching posts - in other words, redundancies. That was all very fair in theory, but, at two forms of entry, Lady Margaret could hardly get smaller without jeopardising its existence. Moreover, the school was heavily oversubscribed; should it not be the less popular schools that bore the brunt? In the end, the Governors simply stood by their existing agreement with the Authority, and continued to admit sixty children a year, while neighbouring schools amalgamated and shrank.

Shortly after Mrs Cairns's arrival, the School lost the good offices of its long-serving Chairman of Governors, the Bishop of Kensington, Ronald Goodchild. His going was to mark a sad break in a tradition as long as the School's history, namely, that the Bishop of Kensington *pro tem.* should be Chairman of Governors. Bishop Goodchild's successor allowed his election to the Governing Body, but resolutely refused to accept the Chairmanship; in fact, he never thereafter attended the meetings, and though his apologies were religiously recorded year after year, it was to be the end of the Kensington connection. In place of Bishop Goodchild, Mr John Muir, of the Education Department, of King's College, London, for many years Vice-Chairman, was unanimously elected. John Muir was an Oxford Classicist, a quietly dignified and peaceable man who steered the Governors equably through many a potentially rough passage. To make good the loss of the Bishop, as far as possible, it was a happy thought, and a revival of a custom as old as the School, to invite the Vicar of St Dionis' (the Rev. Dick Ashton - his daughter Rachel was a pupil) to join the Governors, in November 1982.

The new government lost no time in embarking upon that series of measures that was to transform the education system of this country over the ensuing ten years. The 1980 Education Act began quietly enough, dealing with the composition and conditions of service of Governing Bodies, the process of admissions to secondary schools, and an appeals procedure for parents disappointed in their bid for their child's acceptance at the school of their choice. The Headmistress was well aware of the distress caused to children and parents when they failed to gain admission to Lady Margaret; when the school had embarked upon its comprehensive adventure, it little thought that it would soon become the most popular comprehensive school in the area.

One particular cause of concern for the Governors was the disproportion between the numbers applying within the three "bands" of ability. The ILEA had introduced the banding system to ensure that no school got an unfair number of bright children or less able children. Parents of bright children, aware that Lady Margaret was still, from the waist up, a grammar school, and therefore probably had a more academically orientated staff than the fully comprehensive schools which were their alternatives, plumped for the school in far higher numbers than did the parents of less able children. There were, in the early 1980s, something like two applicants for every place overall; but in Band 1 (the top 25%) the odds were far greater, in Band 2 (the middle 50%) it was about two-to-one, while in Band 3 (the bottom 25%) there were usually hardly enough applicants to fill the quota. In practice, therefore, it was extremely difficult for a clever child to get in, and very easy for the less able. In practice, too, it meant that staunchly Church families were being turned away, while others whose religious affiliations were dubious, to say the least, had to be accepted willy-nilly.

The new Appeals Procedure, with the strong possibility that some disappointed parents would take the Governors to law over the rejection of their child (in theory, as far as the House of Lords!) meant that the admissions criteria had to be tightened up; an immediate casualty was the process of interviewing each child and her parents before acceptance, since this could lead to subjective decisions and charges of prejudice. In the first year of the new system there were nine appeals; but over the years, as the school became more popular, this increased to fifty or more, each one a time-consuming, expensive, and ultimately futile, chasing after places that did not exist.

Extraordinarily, at this juncture (March 1982), the London Diocesan Board approached the School with yet another scheme for the amalgamation of Lady Margaret with St Mark's, as a six-form entry school; neither school evinced any interest in this, and the proposal was dropped.

Further changes continued to occur. The Governors' meeting on January 25th, 1983, voted to accept a fundamental change in the School's recruitment policy. Though a Church school, Lady Margaret had always left the door open for children of other persuasions, or indeed none at all. Since the Act of 1980 and the consequential tightening up of admission criteria, overdue emphasis was being placed, in the view of several of the Governors, on membership of the Church of England. The School, it was felt, should not only be preaching to the converted, but should also fulfil a missionary role. It was decided that half the places offered each year should be designated "Foundation Places", for which only Church of England applications would be accepted, and the other half "Open Places", which would be open to any families to apply for. This system has so far served the School well, and still operates. At their June meeting, another change overtook the Governing Body; for the first time it had on it two Parent Governors and two Teacher Governors. For some time both the Parents" Association and the Staff had sent observers along to the meetings (as indeed, since Miss Cavendish's day, the School, who were represented by the Head Girl and her Deputy), but these observers were not allowed to vote; now, they were to be full members of the Governing Body, with full voting rights.

As the grammar school element gradually worked itself out, so the element of cooperation between Lady Margaret and its neighbours at Sixth Form level grew. Some departments were ahead of others on this; the Geography department, particularly, under its new Head, Mrs Thwaites, had an excellent relationship with the geographers of Henry Compton School, and joint field trips, including four highly successful and exciting trips to Iceland, were organised. Elaine Thwaites, a London MSc, and so no slouch academically, was possessed of an almost frenetic energy, and each of these trips, which were very expensive, would be proceeded by a series of fund-raising activities by which she wrung money from every source available in order to subsidise her students. (It is clear that her own pocket was one of those sources.)

Eventually, by 1982, the time came to formalise the cooperative arrangements, and the Fulham Sixth Form Consortium was established, and soon all the secondary schools of the area were part of it - Lady Margaret, St Mark's, Hurlingham and Chelsea, Henry Compton, Fulham Gilliatt (later Fulham Cross); Jill Rickett, Head of the Mathematics Department, took on the post of Sixth Form Coordinator. Coordination certainly there had to be; the five schools had to synchronise their time-tables to a great extent, since the arrangements involved Sixth Formers attending lessons in each other's schools. The potential disruption by strange pupils, including boys of course, leaving and entering buildings at all times of the day was overcome to some extent by timetabling as few moves as possible; and the security aspects of the scheme were dealt with by issuing an identity card to each student. Nevertheless, it seemed to some that Sixth Formers were spending an inordinate amount of time wandering around Fulham when they might be in the library studying.

An exacerbating feature of the whole scheme was the Tertiary Education Boards (TEBs, as they were acronymically known), a typical piece of ILEA bureaucracy that must have struck some inky official at County Hall as highly reasonable and administratively sound, but which in effect made operating the Consortium a nightmare. TEBs were essentially a cost-cutting device; it was their function to authorise (or not) Sixth Form courses before they could be allowed to run. The Consortium would put in its bids, with projected numbers wishing to take each course, and the TEB would get out its calculator. Its most notorious rule (later modified in self-defence) was that no class could go ahead with fewer than ten students in it. That was fine for popular subjects, but Religious Studies, Spanish, even Physics and Chemistry, often could not raise such numbers, even from five schools. A student would find that he could not do Physics, because it was not being offered. But he needed Physics for his future plans, and so he took himself off to an alternative venue for his "A" levels - one of the Sixth Form Colleges then being set up, an independent school, the London Oratory (which from the beginning played the maverick and refused to have anything to do with the TEBs), or a College of Further Education. The bureaucrat's neat little scheme had made no allowances for the fact that this was not a captive market. Nor was that all, for when the student left, he reduced the numbers in the Mathematics and Chemistry classes; they might then fall below the magic number, and therefore be cut. And so the snowball continued merrily downhill.

Miss Rickett reported to the Governors (November 2nd, 1982) that the Consortium had got off to a good start; a large proportion of its early students were in fact Lady Margaret girls; the first wave (or "cohort", as the new jargon had it) of the comprehensive intake had now reached the Lower Sixth. But there then began a significant decline in the total school role; recruitment at 11 was still good, but it was in the Sixth Form that numbers were dropping. First a trickle, and then a stream, of Fifth Formers decided that they would, reluctantly, prefer to follow their "A" level studies elsewhere. Heartbroken staff would see their best pupils, carefully nurtured over five years for the ultimate glories of the "A" level course, leave them, with regret, with apologies, with tears very often, but with determination. Nor could conscientious teachers reasonably argue that two years at St Paul's (paid for by painful, but mercifully brief, family economies) would not be a considerably better experience than the patchy, peripatetic package offered by the Fulham Consortium. It had been predicted in the Feasibility Study that Sixth Form numbers would go down, because in a comprehensive school a smaller proportion of pupils would be doing "A" levels; but in practice it was the academic pupils who were leaving, and the non-academic ones who were staying.

It did not help that some of the visiting students did not share those graces of life that most Lady Margaret girls had somehow or other picked up in their time at the school. Many of the visitors were excellent people, and good and rewarding friendships grew up between Sixth Formers of different schools. But others were not, and a series of unpleasant incidents soured somewhat the spirit of cooperation within the system; and provided yet another reason for girls to seek their further education elsewhere. Some girls were lucky, and had timetables that kept them almost entirely on the Lady Margaret site. Sophie McLaughlin was one of these, which goes some way to explaining her success.

It was with the few senior girls that were around on the premises that one could pretend that the good days were still with us. It was when the Sixth Form were not around that the School realised what part they had played in the life of the place; and this was one educational experience that had been overlooked. Though the Order continued to exist, the day-to-day duties they had performed had now to be assumed by the Fifth Form, and Prefects were appointed from among their number. The Fifth Form also took over the House Captaincies. This was all very well for the Fifth Form, and it could be argued that they were receiving a valuable lesson in responsibility; but the Sixth Form became, and felt, more and more marginalised, no longer part of the School community. Even their glorious Common Room was taken from them (understandably, because it was so often completely empty, but regrettably), and taken over by the Art department. (Its new Head, Ann Duncan, later Mrs High, was to continue and expand upon the excellent work of Joy Boundy; and Art College continues to figure high on the list of destinations of LMS school-leavers.)

The English Department was one of the few that had enough Sixth Form students of its own that it did not need to "cooperate"; they felt it incumbent on them to do something to "keep things going". In 1983, and again in 1985, the "A" level English class performed a play at the end of the summer term. Sophie McLaughlin and her friends presented *Ages Ago*, a short comic opera by W S Gilbert (with music by Frederic Clay), which was the forerunner (with its portrait gallery coming to life) of his later *Ruddigore*; and three years later a group led by Sarah Baker (daughter of George Baker, of Inspector Wexford fame) presented *A Sensation Novel*, also by Gilbert (with music by Florian Pascal). This involved Sarah, playing Gripper the detective, to don a number of different disguises, involving rapid changes of costume in the wings between appearances. (Sarah went on to read English at Manchester College, in Oxford, where she became much involved in the University Dramatic Society, and seemed set to follow in father's footsteps.)

The continuing teachers' work-to-rule meant that extra-curricular activities such as plays were somewhat proscribed; but there were those who felt strongly that, whatever the justice of the teachers' case, the pupils in the school would only be going through once, and should not miss the opportunities that their predecessors had had. The two short Gilbert pieces, therefore, were supplemented on each occasion by a junior play, Fielding's *Tom Thumb* and that old favourite of the Toy Theatre, *The Miller and his Men*, by Isaac Pocock, complete with pyrotechnic devices in the final explosion of the mill. During this period, too, the musical life of the School flourished, under its new director, Graham Thorp. A Youth and Music group was set up, likewise an Early Music group. The Madrigal Group pursued its successful way, often regaling the School and Staff parties with wickedly satirical pieces of Miss Walhouse's own composition. In the autumn of 1982, Mr Thorp established the Lady Margaret Musical Society, open to girls, Old Girls, parents and friends, which mounted a series of musical events, culminating in a magnificent performance of Handel's *Messiah*.

In 1982, it was decided that the penultimate week of the summer term should be Special Activities Week. (The activities took place in school hours, and were not affected by the work-to-rule.) The comprehensive nature of the school had made several members of the Staff think that the concept of education ought to be broadened, and the horizons of many of the children now coming into the school needed opening up.

> *We held our first Activities Week in the summer of 1982. It happened as a result of several factors. It was felt by many of the Staff that now Lady Margaret was a comprehensive school, it should be catering for a wider interpretation of "education" than the merely academic. There was the yearly problem of what to do with the awkward period following public and school examinations. There were memories among the longer serving teachers of the custom of the early 70s of taking the entire Fifth Form away for a week following the public examinations. The examples of one or two other pioneering schools were known to us as well. And so, in the spring of 1982, with the strong encouragement and enthusiasm of Mrs Cairns, a programme was put together and presented to the school.*
> (Magazine, 1985)

There were no residential trips that first year. The girls, when asked for suggestions and comments, pleaded for these to be included next time. And so they were - camping at Weymouth, touring Norfolk, and Mr Thorp's Music Camp at Mrs Thwaites's wonderful house in Dorset (girls spent the week making music and rehearsing a concert which they gave at the end of the week in Blandford Parish Church.). In 1984, there was an even more adventurous programme - a week in Normandy, another Music Camp, more camping, riding on Dartmoor (a firm favourite ever since), and a trip to the Forest of Dean (this was the fore-runner of Mr Owen's trips to Cornwall and Yorkshire). Those staying in London chose to do "package weeks" - Computers, PE, Business Studies, Cookery, Theatre, Art and Craft, or Touring London. This set the pattern for all subsequent Activities Week, which have become a permanent feature of the school year.

As the mid-eighties approached, the slide in Sixth Form numbers grew steeper. What was more worrying, the number of applications at age 11 began to fall; they had risen to around 180 (for 60 places, be it remembered), but fell back gradually to just over 100. This was still very healthy by most standards, but for Lady Margaret it was worrying. With the decline in "A" level teaching, staff who valued such work were finding their profession less rewarding, and looked elsewhere for fulfilment. There had been a time when teachers had had the same opportunities as doctors to specialise, but the prevailing egalitarian ethos was making such a choice available only in the independent sector, just as in the name of equality the chance to choose a grammar school education was being limited to those with the money to buy it. It was, quite literally, a tearful occasion when Graham Thorp left to take up an independent school post in Guildford; and the school lost yet another highly academic Sixth Former who left to do her "A" level Music elsewhere.

For a number of reasons, therefore, it was a dispiriting time, especially for those who had known Lady Margaret in its heyday. The increasingly bureaucratic interference of County Hall was not designed to help matters. The Authority launched a series of "initiatives", which were imposed in blanket fashion on the schools without distinction. Schools were called upon to make "statements", along the lines of "evil is wrong"; in pursuit of this a School Multi-Ethnic Working Party was set up, and the children and staff bombarded with exhortations to be non-racist and anti-racist (this despite the fact that until then the School had been remarkably free of racist sentiment and racial disharmony). The Hargreaves Report, "Improving Secondary Schools", was an expensively produced document urging schools, by a vast increase in their report-making and paperwork, to improve their "effectiveness" with parents and public. This was followed by a Quinquennial Review, an idea of the ILEA's to help staff be more effective by getting them to spend hours in compiling statements and statistics. Tyrrell Burgess, at the Governors' meeting of June 19th, 1984, pointed out the conflict between what the School was good at and the relentless demand for reports. One felt almost as if the mark of a good teacher was the quality of his paperwork rather than his ability to engage the interest of his classes and to get them through their examinations.

For many Staff and pupils, the saddest change of all was the demise of the Chapel. There was admittedly a lack of space in the school (when had there ever been otherwise?), and, more and more, odd lessons would be held in there - tutorial groups, music groups, Sixth Form classes - so that its function as a quiet place at the heart of the School was lost. The pews were pushed back, and eventually removed altogether and stored on the stage; the altar remained, forlorn, neglected, except occasionally to be used as writing desk, seat, or dump for piles of books. Something real but intangible had been removed from the life of Lady Margaret. It was not Babylon, and there were no available waters, but there were certainly some who sat down and wept.

In the spring of 1984, Mrs Cairns announced her decision to accept the post of Headmistress of Burlington Danes School, a Church of England mixed school in the north of the Borough. In her place, the Governors appointed the long-serving Deputy, Mrs Joan Olivier, as the School's fifth Headmistress.

Little angels!

Parents' Evening.

Beyond

Joan Olivier

The new Headmistress (so she called herself - Mrs Cairns had preferred the style "Head Teacher") had been at the school since 1973, when she took over as Deputy Headmistress from Miss Long. She had some misgivings about applying for the "top job", but was persuaded to do so, and was successful.

Joan Olivier was in her early forties. She had spent her early days in her native Scotland, first at a boarding school which she hated, and then at Morrison's Academy in Crieff. When she was twelve her family had moved south, and she had attended the Rosa Bassett School in Streatham. She read History at London University, and did professional training at Cambridge. She was appointed to the staff of Camden School, and four years later became Head of the History Department. It was from there that she was appointed Deputy Headmistress at Lady Margaret.

To take her place as Deputy, the School appointed its first Deputy Headmaster (or male Deputy Head, to be more logical). Colin Busby was a Fulham man through and through, until it came to the matter of football teams, when, for some unaccountable reason, he preferred Brentford. He was born in the clinic next door to Lady Margaret, and eventually became Head of the Religious Education department at Henry Compton. From there he was appointed to Lady Margaret.

The new Head and Deputy were faced immediately with the worsening situation of the teachers' industrial action. The unwillingness of the Government, and of Sir Keith Joseph, the Education Secretary, to make any significant concessions to the "demands" of the teaching unions, led to increasing bitterness and shorter tempers. "Action" was stepped up, and on several occasions children had to be sent home because teachers had "withdrawn their labour". The two main unions represented in the school, the NUT (National Union of Teachers) and the AMMA (Assistant Masters and Mistresses Association), hardened their attitudes beyond even the positions taken up by their colleagues in neighbouring schools. It was not a happy time.

Many extra-curricular activities were affected by the action; even so, a performance of Mozart's Requiem by the Musical Society took place in March 1985, and a production of *Macbeth* was staged in 1986. Activities Week was not affected, nor were the school journeys that took place in the holidays - a new venture was the Art Historians' trip to Florence in 1986, which was to be repeated in succeeding years.

The Chapel emerged from its ignominious state to resume its previous function; in 1988 it was further beautified by by a stained glass window by Sasha Gadsby (Mrs Ward) (1970-77), who had attended the Central School of Art on leaving Lady Margaret. The window had been presented by the parents of Katherine Skeat (1978-85), who had died of leukemia aged 20 (Katie's father, Robert Skeat, had been Classics master at LMS in the early 1970s), and Sophie Tumber (1986), who had died from a brain haemorrhage in her first term at the School, aged 11. Another welcome return, in 1985, was the School Magazine, which had last appeared in 1980.

The biggest worry, however, because its outcome could materially change the character of the School, was the imminent demise of the Sixth Form, not through any machinations on the part of County Hall, but simply because Lady Margaret girls, by and large, would have nothing to do with the Consortium arrangements. Projected figures by the Head of Sixth Form, Mr Ian Davidson, suggested that by 1987 there might be only thirteen girls in the Sixth Form. The grand scheme of cooperation, carefully devised by the Feasibility Study working party, on all the best evidence then available, was not working in practice.

The Governors were horrified to think that the School would become, not by administrative order, but simply by default, an 11-16 school. It could not be allowed to happen. There were those on the Staff who had never been entirely happy with the Consortium arrangements, and one, unsuccessful, candidate for the post of Head of Sixth who had expressed a desire to "bring the Sixth Form home". Parents and girls were asking in anguished tones why they could not do all their Sixth Form studies at their own school, instead of being, as they saw it, forced to leave.

A small group of Staff volunteered to look into the matter - Miss Andrew, Miss Thomas (Head of Religious Studies), and Mr Owen. The question was, if the School "went it alone", could it produce an acceptable curriculum that would do justice to all its potential Sixth Formers? The three staff conferred, and drew up a document containing their thoughts, reservations, and pious hopes on the matter; this they presented to their colleagues.

Coming back from church: Miles Shillingford (Chairman of Governors), Colin Busby and Jan Wright (Deputy Heads).

We are seeking a VI Form which is as far as possible entirely based at LMS, and certainly one that feels itself to be part of the School, and is seen by the rest of the School to be part of it...

It would attract by the expertise of its teaching, with the likelihood of good to excellent results in examinations, and a first-class record in securing employment for its alumnae; by the opportunity given to continue education in the company of friends made in the course of one's school career and with teachers one knows;...by the knowledge that one is in the hands of people who care whether one sinks or swims, and are ever ready to help, advise, and comfort...

"Three little maids from school are we".

Staff responded, thoughtfully, not unreservedly, but in the main willing to try; the alternative was not to be contemplated. From their replies a Report was drawn up (dated June 25th, 1986) for presentation to the Governors. This spelt out the gravity of the present situation.

While cooperation on this limited scale was in being, there were few problems; girls still spent most of their time at LMS, and could take part in its activities and social life. But already there were signs that all was not well. It started by several of the ablest girls leaving at the end of the Fifth Form, often to spend two years in an independent school VI Form. Then as the consortium arrangements absorbed more and more courses, and included a greater number of schools, this trickle grew considerably larger, until we are faced with the prospect next term of a tiny Upper VI, and a new Lower VI with at most two "A" level candidates in it. If the LMS VI Form survives in its present form, it will consist only of "O" level retakes and CPVE courses. This must in the not very long term have an effect upon the sort of staff that LMS recruits, and therefore upon the teaching of the rest of the school.

The choice was a stark one, and starkly presented. A quick canvass of the current Fifth Form (most of whom were leaving) had revealed that some 75% of them would have stayed had Lady Margaret had its own Sixth Form. This gave hope that if the School would move quickly and decisively on the matter, the present Fourth Form might be saved. The Report outlined how it might be done - mixed Upper and Lower Sixth classes, where appropriate, very limited cooperation with other institutions, a limited number of the most popular non-"A" level courses. On the positive side, the School could offer from its own resources some 15 "A" level courses, as many indeed as the Consortium would be offering, and such a Sixth Form might well attract outsiders into it. It was estimated that the first year of its operation (1987-88) there might be 48 pupils in the Lower Sixth, and the following year (1988-89) there would be a total Sixth Form of about 80. (These figures turned out to be remarkably accurate, far more so than any of the expensively produced projections of numbers put out by County Hall!) It would mean more teaching time for the Staff, but they were prepared to do this rather than continue with the present arrangements.

Car Boot Sale.

The Governors conferred, and agreed to go ahead. (Mr Muir had resigned the Chairmanship on May 13th, 1986, because of his appointment as Vice-Principal of King's College, London, and Tyrrell Burgess, now Professor Burgess, was elected in his place.) The TEB's numbers rule would have to be ignored, but, it was discovered, it was a paper tiger, with no legal validity at all; the Authority were bound to fund the School on the pupils it had, and could not dictate to the Governors how the School should be organised internally. Lady Margaret gave notice that it was pulling out of the Consortium; and though there were earnest pleas from the ILEA to change its mind (the promise of a wonderful Sixth Form Centre in Fulham was dangled before the Governors to dissuade them from their course of action), the School went ahead with the venture.

The subsequent history of the Sixth Form speaks for itself. Of the pioneer year (1987-89), nine entered University courses, ten other further education courses, and the rest employment or training of a worthwhile nature; Louise Moore, who had in fact left from the Fifth Form the year before to attend another school, returned to Lady Margaret to take advantage of the new regime, and gained a place at Somerville College, Oxford, to read Law. Over the next three years, there were to be two more Oxford entrants (Marylois Chan and Naomi Hossain) and one at Cambridge (Joy Wheeler), besides numbers of other university, art college, and polytechnic successes. By 1990, the numbers had risen to almost ninety, and this year (1992) we are expecting for the first time a significant number of entrants from outside the school. The latest "A" level results (1992) show that as many students are gaining "A" levels as when Lady Margaret was a grammar school, and over 50% of them in the higher grades. (One remarkable development not envisaged when the venture was contemplated is the significant number of students who, classified as Band 2, and in one case, Band 3, actually gained "A" level passes.)

Marylois Chan and Natasha Imison hard at work.

83

Sixth Form leavers' Eucharist in the garden, June 1992.

Sixth Form leavers' Breakfast, June 1992.

Irene Lovett - Mrs Eric Fraser - 75 years on! 18th March 1992.

The "new" Sixth Form were on parade for the School's 70th Birthday, in 1987, dressed in Edwardian costume as far as possible; it was, one recalls, a particularly happy occasion. The afternoon of the Birthday had been billed as an educational lecture from a guest speaker. The whole School dutifully filed into the Hall, where some old buffer proceeded to bore them rigid with a mass of mumbled statistics read from a book. After ten minutes, Mrs Olivier could stand no more; she stood up and stopped the speaker, telling him she had never heard an address so awful. The polite young ladies of Lady Margaret were horrified - not at the speaker, but at the Headmistress's audacity! But it was all an elaborate hoax; the curtains opened, and the Staff performance of *Cinderella* took the stage. It was, indeed, a particularly happy occasion.

There loomed on the scene now the Education Act of 1988, which with its successors, was to have significant effects upon Lady Margaret, as upon all other schools. Schools could now "opt out" of local government control and become Grant Maintained Schools, funded directly from the Department of Education and Science, and with full control over their finances. All schools were made much more responsible in this field by the introduction of Local Management of Schools (confusingly abbreviated to "LMS"), which gave every school control of 85% of its total budget; staff salaries, building and decorating, as well as the purchase of day-to-day equipment, would now be the responsibility of head teachers and governors, rather than the local authority. The schools were being set free in one sense, perhaps, but burdened by the weight of decision-making that was now thrust upon them.

The introduction of the National Curriculum, hardly a pause for breath after the assimilation of the new GCSE examination which had replaced the GCE "O" level and the CSE in 1989, meant an enormous burden of revising working practices for already overloaded teachers. The industrial action of a few years earlier had faded away, and the Government seemed determined that a punch-drunk profession would not have the energy, nor indeed the legal scope, to impose restrictive practices again. Terms and conditions of employment were spelt out, job descriptions drawn up, and the old days of professional understanding of what it was to be a teacher seemed gone for ever.

The recent White Paper (July 1992) sets out the Government's determination to encourage all secondary schools to become Grant-Maintained, and so marginalise the schools' relationship with the local authorities. (Upon the demise of the ILEA in March, 1990, Lady Margaret had become the resonsibility of the London Borough of Hammersmith and Fulham.) If the School takes that road, the wheel would have come full circle, for it would then be in a position very similar to its original state, except that it would be publicly funded, and, of course, subject to the National Curriculum. But of recent events I make but brief mention; their considered history will be the task of whoever writes the revision of this book for the 100th Birthday in 2017.

The School would appear to have recovered from its malaise of just six years ago. The Sixth Form initiative seems to have been a success. Applications at age 11 are the highest in the School's history, approaching 300 (for 66 places); with the end of "banding", Lady Margaret has introduced its own entrance test, not in order to choose the best 66, but in order to maintain its comprehensive intake. Cultural life flourishes, with performances of *Trial by Jury, The Mikado, The Boy Friend*, as well as regular concerts; the Sixth Form began in 1991 what they hoped would become a tradition, that the Lower Sixth (or Year 12, as it now is under the new National Curriculum numbering system) would each year produce a play - they began with the horror parody *Dracula is Undead and Well, and Living in Purfleet*. The School has featured in two national newspaper surveys as among the best in the country, both for its examination results and its popularity with parents. The recent visit of Her Majesty's Inspectors (March 1991) used words such as "outstanding" and "excellent" about several aspects of the School. For instance:

> *The standards of behaviour in the school are excellent. Relationships between teachers and pupils and among the girls themselves are characterised by genuine warmth, courtesy and respect . . . . They also value each other, both in contributions to lessons and around the school . . . The pupils hold a positive view of the school; they feel valued by the staff and each other..*

Much of the credit for the excellence of this Report must go to the sterling work of the staff.

In the final analysis, schools are about people; and that was brought home to many not more clearly than when, on Foundation Day 1992, 89-year-old Mrs Fraser, Irene Lovett as was, "a very clever LCC child", as Enid Moberly Bell had called her back in 1917, one of the original Sixth Form who had started school at Whitelands, and who was "rescued" by Miss Lupton's generosity, stood on the platform in the Hall and spoke, without notes, and as clear as a bell, of the School she loved, and which had shaped her life. To her, and all her fellow Lady Margaret girls, this history is dedicated.